The Explanation of the Chapters on

Repentance
& the Prohibition
of backbiting &
Talebearing

First Edition: 2015

ISBN: 978-1-910015-07-0

Printed and Distributed by:

Darussalam International Publications Ltd.
Leyton Business Centre
Unit-17, Etloe Road, Leyton, London, E10 7BT
Tel: 0044 208539 4885   Fax: 00442085394889
Website: www.darussalam.com
Email: info@darussalam.com

Cover design, editing and typesetting by:
Abū Fātimah Azhar Majothī
www.ihsaandesign.com

THE EXPLANATION OF THE CHAPTERS ON

REPENTANCE & THE PROHIBITION OF BACKBITING & TALEBEARING

From the Classical Collection of Hadith
Riyaadh As-Saaliheen by Imam An-Nawawi

Explained by the Esteemed Shaykh,
and Reviver of the Sunnah,
Shaykh Muhammad Ibn Saalih Uthaymeen ﷺ

Translated and Summarised by
Taalib Ibn Tyson Al-Britaani

DARUSSALAM
GLOBAL LEADER IN ISLAMIC BOOKS
Riyadh • Jeddah • Al-Khobar • Sharjah • Lahore • London • Houston • New York

بسم الله الرحمن الرحيم

CONTENTS

باب التوبة

THE CHAPTER ON REPENTANCE

The Scholars say: it is necessary to repent from every sin. If the offence involves the right of Allah, not a human, then there are three conditions to be met in order for that repentance to be accepted by Allah:

1. To desist from committing it.
2. To feel sorry for committing it.
3. To decide not to recommit it.

Any repentance failing to meet any of these three conditions would not be sound. But if the sin involves a person's right, it requires a fourth condition, i.e., to absolve oneself from the owner's right. If it is property, he should return it to its rightful owner. If it is slandering or backbiting, one should seek pardon from the offended.

One should also repent from all sins. If he repents from some, his repentance would still be sound according to the people of sound knowledge. He should, however, repent from the rest. Scriptural proofs from the Book and the Sunnah and the consensus of the Scholars support the obligation of repentance.

Allah the Exalted says in the Quran:

وَتُوبُوٓا۟ إِلَى ٱللَّهِ جَمِيعًا أَيُّهَ ٱلْمُؤْمِنُونَ لَعَلَّكُمْ تُفْلِحُونَ

"And all of you beg Allah to forgive you, O believers, that you may be successful." (An-Noor, 31)

Also Allah the Exalted says:

وَأَنِ ٱسْتَغْفِرُوا۟ رَبَّكُمْ ثُمَّ تُوبُوٓا۟ إِلَيْهِ

"Seek the forgiveness of your Lord, and turn to Him in repentance." (Al-Hood, 3)

The Exalted also says:

يَـٰٓأَيُّهَا ٱلَّذِينَ ءَامَنُوا۟ تُوبُوٓا۟ إِلَى ٱللَّهِ تَوْبَةً نَّصُوحًا

"O you who believe! Turn to Allah with sincere repentance." (At-Tahreem, 8)

[EXPLANATION OF CHAPTER HEADING AND SUPPORTING VERSES]

Linguistically, *Tawbah*, or repentance, means to renounce a certain matter. In the Sharia, it refers to the act of returning from the disobedience of Allah the Exalted to His obedience. What is considered and counted as the greatest type of repentance, as well as the most compulsory, is from Kufr (disbelief in Allah) to Emaan (belief and faith in Allah), as Allah ﷻ says in the Qur'an:

قُل لِّلَّذِينَ كَفَرُوٓاْ إِن يَنتَهُواْ يُغْفَرْ لَهُم مَّا قَدْ سَلَفَ

"Say to those who disbelieve, if they cease (from disbelief) their past will be forgiven." (Al-Anfaal, 38)

The third type of repentance is from minor sins.

So the act of seeking repentance is deemed obligatory from every sin committed. For an individual's repentance to be accepted, then there are three conditions, as the author states, but after review, there are in fact five:

The First Condition: That is, an individual repents sincerely and whole-heartedly to Allah alone. If this is done, Allah will surely turn to him in forgiveness. It should not be done to show off or to please the people so as to gain closeness to them, or as a means to prevent harm befalling him from the ruler or those in authority. Rather, an individual does so seeking the pleasure of Allah and the next life. If the repentance is done in this way, as we said, Allah will overlook the servant's faults.

The Second Condition: The individual regrets committing that sinful act, which is a sure indication that his (her) repentance was truthful, and this means, the individual was sad and grieved over committing that wrongdoing. So the individual realises he has fallen short, and will not free himself from that sin until he repents to Allah.

The Third Condition: The individual discontinues the disobedience, and this is the most important of all the conditions. For example, if an individual has abandoned one of the obligatory deeds, such as not paying his Zakaat, if this person now wants to repent to Allah, he would have to pay that Zakaat and that which he has previously fallen short in paying. If the individual is falling short regarding his dealings and bad treatment towards his parents, then in this case he starts treating them in a good and correct manner. Also if an individual has cut ties with his (her) parent, similarly he would have to mend that relationship and maintain ties with them. Just like the individual who falls short and commits any of the forbidden acts, then right away he should abstain from it.

Likewise, if the servant's sin is lying, cheating or not fulfilling any trust assigned to him (her), it becomes a must upon him to also give that act up; say if he was acquiring wealth in an unlawful way, then it becomes obligatory upon him to return that wealth he has amassed to its rightful owner to become absolutely absolved from that wronged individual.

To add to this, if the individual has fallen into backbiting any particular individual or he reviled them, in this case, if he wanted to repent from that act, he must completely abandon and give up that action; if this individual repents but persists upon that act while remaining repentant, then this type of repentance yields little fruit and is not accepted. Rather, this considered as a mere mockery of Allah ﷻ. How can one claim to have repented to Allah, but at the same time continue to commit the wrong action he claims to have repented from! For example, say you wronged an individual and then apologised to him, saying "I am very sorry and feel great remorse for my behaviour! Please forgive me and I will no longer wrong you" but your intention differs, and in your heart you say: I will wrong him again for what I have apologised to him for! So if such a person is counted as making fun of that individual, then what would be case with regards to Allah the Lord of the worlds? We say, in reality the repentant one is he who gives up committing the sin he is embarking upon.

It is strange what some people do; for instance, you sit with them and they express complete dislike for Riba (interest) but at the same time, they yearn for it, and we seek refuge with Allah from this! Similarly, an individual claims to hate backbiting and slandering others, but at the same time this individual is one of the worst backbiters! We ask Allah for good health! Or an individual claims to have forsaken lying and being dishonest regarding people's trust, but he is from the worst type of liars and dishonest individuals that always seems to break their trusts among the people.

In short, it is an obligation upon the Muslim, if he wants to turn towards Allah in Repentance, to firstly give up that sin he is repenting from, as not doing so and persisting upon that sin while repenting is rejected and not accepted by Allah.

If the wrongdoing is merely between the servant and Allah, then it is enough to for the servant to give up that wrongdoing as well as repent to Allah;, and an individual is forbidden to talk about that sin he repented from, whatsoever that sin or wrongdoing may be, as this sin was between him and Allah and He honoured that individual by concealing the sin that this individual committed from the people's eyes and ears. So do not let anyone know what sin you have committed that you repented to Allah from, just as the Prophet ﷺ said:

كُلُّ أُمَّتِي مُعَافًى إِلاَّ الْمُجَاهِرِينَ

"Every one of my followers will be forgiven except those who expose (openly) their wrongdoings.

Another matter which is considered exposing one's wrongdoings is related in another narration of the Prophet ﷺ when he said:

أَنْ يَفْعَلَ الذَّنْبَ ثُمَّ يُصْبِح يُحَدِّث بِهِ النَّاس يقول فَعَلْتُ كَذَا وَكَذَا

"The slave commits a sin, then in the morning he says to the people I committed such-and-such sin."

Regarding this matter at hand, some of the scholars have given exceptional cases and of them is if an individual commits a wrongdoing that entails the prescribed punishment, then in this case it is allowed for him to present himself to those in authority who deliver such types of punishments if he wants to purify himself from such a sin, but we say that in such case, it would be better for such individuals to not do this, rather, refrain and conceal such wrongdoings. And what we mean is, it is allowed for an individual to present himself to those in authority if they have indulged in one of major wrongdoings that entails one of the prescribed punishments such as Zina (fornication) and the likes, and that is he (she) says, "I have committed this or that wrongdoing," requesting that those in authority deliver the prescribed punishment as a means of expiation.

As for other types of sins, it would be much better to conceal them from those in authority as Allah has concealed them also from others. And this also includes Zina and the likes, so one should not expose them to any individuals at all, whosoever they may be. Surely Allah the Exalted forgives the repentant one and overlooks their faults.

On the other hand we say, if the wrongdoing was committed against one of the creation, regarding wealth for example, then in this case, Allah will not accept one's repentance until that individual restores the wealth to its rightful owner.

But if this is not possible, maybe due to not knowing the victim's whereabouts or location, then the wrongdoer should give away that amount in charity to free himself from that wealth. For certainly Allah ﷻ knows their whereabouts and He will restore it to them.

But if possible, the wrongdoer must go to that individual and absolve himself from that wrongdoing. So for instance, if you wrongfully struck an individual on his back, then in this case you should request from them to also strike your back equally. Wherever you have struck him, you allow him to hit you likewise, and the proof for this is the statement of Allah the Exalted in the Qur'an when He says:

$$\text{وَجَزَٰٓؤُاْ سَيِّئَةٖ سَيِّئَةٞ مِّثۡلُهَا}$$

"The recompense for evil is an evil like thereof."
(Ash-Shura, 40)

14

Also Allah the Exalted says:

فَمَنِ ٱعْتَدَىٰ عَلَيْكُمْ فَٱعْتَدُوا۟ عَلَيْهِ بِمِثْلِ مَا ٱعْتَدَىٰ عَلَيْكُمْ

"Then whoever transgresses the prohibition against you, you transgress likewise against him." (Al-Baqarah 194)

And if it is related to reviling, abusing or cursing that individual by statement then, in this case, one is obligated to go to that individual, and seek his forgiveness, and say for instance, that victim demands wealth from the one who has wronged him, in this case the wrongdoer should give him the amount he requested (within reason).

If one backbites an individual and wants to repent from that act, then the scholars differing regarding this matter, and what to do pertaining to its expiation; some say it is a requirement to actually go to that individual one has backbitten and say: "O so and so! I have said such-and-such words about you, please forgive me for what I have uttered regarding you!" Other scholars have said: No! The issue needs elaboration, and one should not just go to that individual one has backbitten; rather they say in clarifying the matter: if the backbitten one knows you have backbitten him, then in this case, it becomes a must to go to him and request his forgiveness. But on the other hand if he is unaware an individual his backbitten him, then it this case one it is not required to go to him, rather, they should ask Allah to forgive (that individual's) wrongdoings as well as mention something good regarding him in the same gathering in which he had first spoken wrongly of him, as undoubtedly, good deeds wipe away bad deeds. And from the many views regarding this issue, the last view seems to be the strongest and most correct view. And regarding seeking forgiveness for the individual, then it is by saying: "O Allah forgive so-and-so." And this is in accordance with the narration about the expiation for backbiting an individual, which states: "The expiation for backbiting an individual is seeking forgiveness from him (or her)." In short, for the repentance of an individual to be accepted, then that individual has to return the wronged one's rights.

The Fourth Condition (of Repentance): The individual resolves never to return to the act. But let's say the individual intends, that if he has a chance in the future to recommit that sin again, then he will do so. If this is the case, then this individual's repentance is not accepted. For example, an individual uses his wealth to commit a wrongdoing, say to purchase alcohol, and he goes to another country to obtain this as well as to commit Zina, and we seek Allah's refuge from this; let's say this individual is afflicted with poverty, so due to this he says: "O Allah I ask You to forgive me!" So this individual utters these words but at the same time this individual is lying, and within his intention he says, if he ever becomes wealthy again he will commit the exact same wrongdoing he is repenting from! In this case, such repentance is invalid! Whether or not such an individual repents or not, it is only his financial difficulties that are preventing him from recommitting such wrongdoings. And many individuals are afflicted with poverty, so when this occurs they then say: "I (will now) give up such-and-such wrongdoing!" But within their hearts, they yearn and want to recommit that same sin at the next available chance they get.

The Fifth Condition: The repentance one makes is at that time when it is accepted, for if an individual repents at the wrong time then it will be rejected, and this is based on the following two reasons:

As for the first, then it is specific, which is related to just that individual. That is - an individual makes repentance before his life comes to an end. And this means before death overtakes him; Allah ﷺ says in the Qur'an:

وَلَيْسَتِ ٱلتَّوْبَةُ لِلَّذِينَ يَعْمَلُونَ ٱلسَّيِّئَاتِ حَتَّىٰ إِذَا حَضَرَ أَحَدَهُمُ

ٱلْمَوْتُ قَالَ إِنِّى تُبْتُ ٱلْـَٰٔنَ

"And no effect is the Repentance of those who continue to do evil deeds until death faces one of them and he says: 'Now I repent.'" (An-Nisaa', 18)

So there is no repentance for this individual! Allah the Exalted also says:

فَلَمَّا رَأَوْاْ بَأْسَنَا قَالُوٓاْ ءَامَنَّا بِٱللَّهِ وَحْدَهُۥ وَكَفَرْنَا بِمَا كُنَّا بِهِۦ

مُشْرِكِينَ • فَلَمْ يَكُ يَنفَعُهُمْ إِيمَٰنُهُمْ لَمَّا رَأَوْاْ بَأْسَنَا ۖ سُنَّتَ ٱللَّهِ ٱلَّتِى

قَدْ خَلَتْ فِى عِبَادِهِۦ ۖ وَخَسِرَ هُنَالِكَ ٱلْكَٰفِرُونَ

"So when they saw Our Punishment, they said: 'We believe in Allah Alone and reject (all) that we used to associate with Him as (His) partners.' Then their faith (in Islamic Monotheism) could not avail them when they saw Our punishment; (like) this has been

the way of Allah in dealing with His slaves. And there the disbelievers lost utterly (when Our torment covered them)."(Al-Ghaafir, 84-85)

So an individual has to view death as something that can occur at any given moment, and he should never give into despair and delay his repentance from its accepted time.

The second type is general, and what is intended by that, is clarified by the statement of the Prophet (Muhammad) ﷺ, who said:

لَا تَنْقَطِعُ الهِجْرَةُ حَتَّى تَنْقَطِعَ التَّوْبَةُ , وَلَا تَنْقَطِعُ التَّوْبَةُ حَتَّى تَطْلُعَ الشَّمْسُ مِن مَغْرِبِها

"Hijrah will not cease until repentance ceases (to be accepted). And repentance will not cease (to be accepted) until the sun rises from the place where it sets (i.e. the west)."

So if the sun rises from the west, repentance will not be of any avail to the repentant one as Allah the Exalted has stated:

هَلْ يَنظُرُونَ إِلَّا أَن تَأْتِيَهُمُ ٱلْمَلَـٰئِكَةُ أَوْ يَأْتِيَ رَبُّكَ أَوْ يَأْتِيَ بَعْضُ ءَايَـٰتِ رَبِّكَ ۗ يَوْمَ يَأْتِي بَعْضُ ءَايَـٰتِ رَبِّكَ لَا يَنفَعُ نَفْسًا إِيمَـٰنُهَا لَمْ تَكُنْ ءَامَنَتْ مِن قَبْلُ أَوْ كَسَبَتْ فِي إِيمَـٰنِهَا خَيْرًا ۗ قُلِ ٱنتَظِرُوٓا۟ إِنَّا مُنتَظِرُونَ

"Or that some of the Signs of your Lord should come, that day some of the Signs of your Lord do come, no good will it do to a person to believe then,

if he believed not before, nor earned good through his Faith." (Al-An'aam, 158)

This is after the sun rises from the west as the Prophet ﷺ has explained.

The scholars differ regarding the acceptance of an individual's repentance when that individual persists upon another sin. There are three different opinions:

1. Some say yes, it is accepted, and that is if an individual repents from one sin while he is persisting upon another sin, and this individual will incur upon himself the sin for that wrongdoing he is not repenting from it.

2. Others say no, it is not accepted while one persists upon another sin or wrongdoing.

3. While others say this matter needs clarification: if an individual repents from a particular sin but remains persistent upon another sin which is from the same kind of sin, then in this case that repentance itself is not accepted. But if the two sins are different in kind, then the repentance is accepted.

    An example of this is: an individual makes repentance from Riba (interest) but at the same this individual is committing Zina or drinking alcohol, some scholars say, in this case, such repentance is rejected! For how can one consider himself as having repented while still indulging in other wrongdoings? While other scholars say: rather such repentance will be accepted, as Riba is one thing and drinking alcohol is something else. And this, among the many views, is

19

what the author (Imam An-Nawawi) ﷺ himself holds to be the correct view.

In conclusion, the correct view is that yes, one's repentance is accepted while persisting up another sin, but, in saying this, such an individual is not given the title of being the truly repentant one (*At-Ta'ib*), nor praised with this title either, as such an individual has not completely given up his (her) sinful ways, so his repentance is not a complete one, rather, it is deficient. This is the view I myself feel satisfied with and what I incline towards.

The author mentions evidence from the Qur'an and Sunnah indicating the obligation of repentance from all types of wrong committed, and for sure he (Imam An-Nawawi) spoke the truth, as this is what the Qur'an and Sunnah encourages and highlights.

Allah ﷻ clarifies that He loves the repentant and those who keep themselves pure and clean, so this means He the Exalted loves those who persist in repenting to Him verbally and every time they fall into wrongdoing they turn to Him seeking His forgiveness. The author mentions the statement of the Exalted when He says:

$$\text{وَتُوبُوٓا۟ إِلَى ٱللَّهِ جَمِيعًا أَيُّهَ ٱلْمُؤْمِنُونَ لَعَلَّكُمْ تُفْلِحُونَ}$$

"And all of you beg Allah to forgive you, O believers, that you may be successful." (An-Noor 31)

Allah the Exalted mentions this after commanding the believers to lower their gazes in His ﷻ statement:

قُل لِّلْمُؤْمِنِينَ يَغُضُّوا مِنْ أَبْصَرِهِمْ وَيَحْفَظُوا فُرُوجَهُمْ ذَلِكَ أَزْكَىٰ لَهُمْ إِنَّ ٱللَّهَ خَبِيرٌ بِمَا يَصْنَعُونَ • وَقُل لِّلْمُؤْمِنَتِ يَغْضُضْنَ مِنْ أَبْصَرِهِنَّ وَيَحْفَظْنَ فُرُوجَهُنَّ وَلَا يُبْدِينَ زِينَتَهُنَّ إِلَّا مَا ظَهَرَ مِنْهَا وَلْيَضْرِبْنَ بِخُمُرِهِنَّ عَلَىٰ جُيُوبِهِنَّ وَلَا يُبْدِينَ زِينَتَهُنَّ إِلَّا لِبُعُولَتِهِنَّ أَوْ ءَابَآئِهِنَّ أَوْ ءَابَآءِ بُعُولَتِهِنَّ أَوْ أَبْنَآئِهِنَّ أَوْ أَبْنَآءِ بُعُولَتِهِنَّ أَوْ إِخْوَٰنِهِنَّ أَوْ بَنِي إِخْوَٰنِهِنَّ أَوْ بَنِي أَخَوَٰتِهِنَّ أَوْ نِسَآئِهِنَّ أَوْ مَا مَلَكَتْ أَيْمَٰنُهُنَّ أَوِ ٱلتَّٰبِعِينَ غَيْرِ أُوْلِي ٱلْإِرْبَةِ مِنَ ٱلرِّجَالِ أَوِ ٱلطِّفْلِ ٱلَّذِينَ لَمْ يَظْهَرُوا عَلَىٰ عَوْرَٰتِ ٱلنِّسَآءِ وَلَا يَضْرِبْنَ بِأَرْجُلِهِنَّ لِيُعْلَمَ مَا يُخْفِينَ مِن زِينَتِهِنَّ وَتُوبُوٓا إِلَى ٱللَّهِ جَمِيعًا أَيُّهَ ٱلْمُؤْمِنُونَ لَعَلَّكُمْ تُفْلِحُونَ

"And tell the believing men to lower their gaze (from looking at forbidden things), and protect their private parts (from illegal sexual acts, etc.). That is purer for them. Verily, Allah is All-Aware of what they do. And tell the believing women to lower their gaze (from looking at forbidden things), and protect their private parts (from illegal sexual acts, etc.) and not to show off their adornment except only that which is apparent, and to draw their veils all over Juyubihanna (i.e. their bodies, faces necks and bosoms, etc.) and not to reveal their adornment except to their husbands, their fathers, their husbands fathers, theirs sons, their husband's sons, their brothers or their brother's sons, or their sister's sons, or their (Muslim) women (i.e. their sisters in Islam), or the (female) slaves whom their right hands possess, or old male servants who lack vigour, or small children who have no sense of the shame of sex. And let them not stamp their feet so as to reveal what they hide of their adornment. And all of beg Allah to forgive you all, O believers, that you may be successful." (An-Noor, 30-31)

So this is proof that an individual most repent from the unlawful glance at what is forbidden, and not preserving one's private parts, is not restraining the glance from that which is forbidden, for indeed this leads to one's sure destruction, misery and many other calamities, as well as a great trial, as confirmed when the Prophet ﷺ said:

ما تَركْتُ بَعْدِي فِتْنَةً هِيَ أَضَرُّ عَلَى الرِّجالِ مِنَ النِّساء

"I am not leaving behind me a more harmful trial for men than women."

So for this reason you will find our enemies from the Jews, Christians and polytheists, etc. and also those who blindly follow them, trying their hardest to make women the Muslim's downfall! They encourage the woman to walk the streets near-naked, they invite to the mixing of the two sexes, male and female, and they prompt and incite (the women) to indecent lewd behaviour, which is done through words, films and deeds, and we seek refuge with Allah from such things! So we must remember and not forget, the great influence the women has upon even our strong-minded youth, who with regret, are badly affected by some of them, and this is what the Prophet ﷺ mentioned when he said in a narration:

مَا رَأَيْتُ مِنْ نَاقِصَاتِ عَقْلٍ وَدِينٍ أَذْهَبَ لِلُبِّ الْحَازِمِ مِنْ إِحْدَاكُنَّ

"I have not seen any one deficient in intelligence and religion than you. A cautious sensible man could be lead astray by some of you..."

Do we need anything more clearer than this? So if this is the case, that a cautious sensible man can be so easily led astray, what would be the case with those less than this! Those who have but little firmness, a lack of resolve, little religion or manhood if any at all! We say, for sure they certainly will be afflicted even more badly, and we seek refuge with Allah. So this is a sure reality, and for this reason Allah the Exalted commanded the lowering of the gaze:

وَتُوبُوٓا۟ إِلَى ٱللَّهِ جَمِيعًا أَيُّهَ ٱلْمُؤْمِنُونَ لَعَلَّكُمْ تُفْلِحُونَ

"And all of you beg Allah to forgive you, O believers, that you may be successful." (An-Noor 31)

So it becomes a must upon us to encourage each other to repent to Allah ﷻ and not to be lax in this matter.

In this verse, Allah addresses all the Muslims collectively in His saying: **"And all of you beg Allah to forgive you all, O believers"** Regarding Allah's words: **"That you may be successful."** This is proof that indicates that repentance is one of the reasons that lead to success, and the scholars of tafsir have said that **"success"** in the language is comprehensive and means: what is sought after is obtained and what is feared and disliked is fled from and avoided. For sure, man longs, desires and searches for that which is counted as good as well as in the next life and even the disbeliever desires that too, but some are granted this and some are not granted that which is sought after. Regarding the disbeliever, then that which he seeks to acquire, are those things related to this worldly life, as his lifestyle is somewhat similar to a wild beast merely eating, drinking and procreating and no more than that, and he is considered from the worst types of creature in Allah's sight as the Exalted and High says:

$$إِنَّ شَرَّ ٱلدَّوَآبِّ عِندَ ٱللَّهِ ٱلَّذِينَ كَفَرُواْ فَهُمْ لَا يُؤْمِنُونَ$$

"Verily, the worse of moving (living) creatures in the Sight of Allah are those who disbelieve; and they shall not believe." (Al-Anfaal, 55)

The disbeliever is counted among the worse moving creatures on the face of the earth, but even still, he desires those things in this life which are good such as luxury, wellbeing and comfort and all these things are mere matters related to this earthly life. And these things are what he considers his main purpose in life, in a make-believe heaven. And we seek Allah's refuge from this, and also from His Wrath, Punishment and His Hell-fire! In conclusion every individual in life strives for ultimate success, but achieving it all boils down to what he considers what is most important in his life. Lastly we say, for sure repentance leads to that, and that is success, and surely Allah grant success.

[Hadith 13]

Abu Hurairah ﷺ reported the Messenger of Allah ﷺ as saying:

« واللهِ إِنِّي لَأَسْتَغْفِرُ اللهَ ، وَأَتُوبُ إِلَيْهِ ، فِي اليَوْمِ ، أَكثر مِنْ سَبْعِين مَرَّةً » رواه البخاري .

"By Allah, I seek forgiveness and repent to Him more than seventy times a day." [Al-Bukhari]

[Hadith 14]

Al-Agharr ibn Yaasir Al-Muzani ﷺ narrated that the Messenger of Allah ﷺ said:

« يا أَيُّها النَّاس تُوبُوا إِلى اللهِ واستغْفِرُوهُ فإِني أَتوبُ في اليَوْم مائة مَرَّة » رواه مسلم .

"O People! Turn in repentance to Allah and beg pardon of Him. I turn to Him in repentance a hundred times a day." [Muslim]

[EXPLANATION OF HADITHS 13 AND 14]

As is known, the more evidence a thing has, then that surely strengthens and emphasises the thing being mentioned. So the first of these two supporting narrations is that of Abu Hurairah, and regarding it we say: it explains how the Prophet ﷺ acted (seeking Allah forgiveness) even though Allah the Exalted had forgiven all his past and future sins.

In these two narrations is a proof for the following:

A clear indication of the obligation of repentance and that is found in the Prophet's ﷺ saying: "O People! Turn in repentance to Allah!"

One acquires the two following benefits when he repents to Allah:

The First Benefit: Complying and obeying the commandments of Allah the Exalted and the Prophet (Muhammad) ﷺ, and undoubtedly doing so leads to much good, and that good is in this life as well as in the next.

The Second Benefit: Imitating and following the sound and outstanding character of the Prophet ﷺ, whereby he used to repent to Allah a hundred times a day, and this is done by saying:

أَتُوبُ إِلَى اللهِ أَتُوبُ إِلَى اللهِ

"I turn to You (O Allah) in repentance; I turn to You in repentance."

Repentance has to be done with truthfulness, and the repentant one is required to give up the wrongdoing he is committing. As for when the repentance is merely uttered while one's heart yearns to commit that wrongdoing, then this is considered mere mockery of Allah the Exalted, and such repentance is outright rejected.

An in these two narrations is a proof indicating the Prophet (Muhammad) ﷺ was the most devout of all people in his worship towards Allah ﷻ, as well as the most God-fearing, most pious and most knowledgeable of people regarding Him.

And also from these narrations is a proof that the Prophet ﷺ never taught by mere clarification. Rather he taught by way of his actions too; he ﷺ used to seek Allah's forgiveness so as to be a role-model for the people to follow, and he would order them to do so likewise. So from this we see how He advised his Ummah. From us knowing this, it becomes mandated upon us to follow his ﷺ footsteps and commands, and we should be the first to actualise whatsoever he commands. Likewise, whenever the Prophet ﷺ forbids something, we should be from the first among the people to refrain from that matter, as this is from the best of ways in calling people back to Allah - that we are the first to fulfil his commandments, as this was the way the Prophet ﷺ was: he commanded the people to repent and at the same time he himself repented to Allah. So we ask Allah the Exalted to accept our repentance and yours and to guide us and also you to the straight path, for sure Allah grants success!

[Hadith 15]

Anas bin Maalik ﷺ, the servant of the Messenger of Allah ﷺ, narrated: the Messenger of Allah ﷺ said:

لَلَّهُ أَفْرَحُ بِتَوْبِةِ عَبْدِهِ مِنْ أَحَدِكُمْ سقطَ عَلَى بعيرِهِ وقد أَضلَّهُ في أَرضٍ فَلاةٍ متفقٌ عليه.

"Verily, Allah is more delighted with the repentance of His slave than a person who lost his camel in a desert land and then finds it (unexpectedly)." [Agreed Upon]

In another version of Muslim, he said:

« لَلَّهُ أَشدُّ فرحاً بِتَوْبِةِ عَبْدِهِ حِينَ يتُوبُ إِلَيْهِ مِنْ أَحَدِكُمْ كان عَلَى راحِلتِهِ بِأَرْضٍ فلاةٍ ، فانْفلتتْ مِنْهُ وعلَيْها طعامُهُ وشرَابُهُ فأَيِسَ مِنْها ، فأَتَى شَجَرَةً فاضْطَجَعَ في ظِلِّها ، وقد أَيِسَ مِنْ رَاحِلتِهِ ، فَبَيْنما هوَ كذَلِكَ إِذْ هُوَ بِها قَائِمة عِنْدَهُ ، فأَخذ بِخِطامِها ثُمَّ قَالَ مِنْ شِدَّةِ الفَرِحِ: اللَّهُمَّ أنت عبْدِي وأَنا رَبُّكَ، أخْطأَ مِنْ شِدَّةِ الفرح » .

"Verily, Allah is more pleased with the repentance of His slave than a person who has his camel in a waterless desert carrying his provision of food and drink and it gets lost. Having lost all hopes (to get that camel back), the man lies down in shade and is disappointed about his camel; when all of a sudden he finds the camel standing before him. He takes hold of its reins and then out of boundless joy blurts out: 'O Allah, You are my slave and I am your Lord!' He commits this mistake out of extreme joy."

[EXPLANATION OF HADITH 15]

It is narrated from Anas ﷺ that the Prophet said: "Verily, Allah is more pleased with the Repentance of His slave than a person who has his camel in a waterless desert carrying his provision of food and drink and it is lost." This explains that there was an individual in a particular land, wherein there was no water, food or inhabitants, and his riding beast got lost. So he goes in search of it but fails to find it, and retreats to a nearby tree to take rest awaiting death. Undergoing all of this, he awakes from this state, and before his very eyes is the same riding beast that he had given up all hope in ever finding. Surely, he is over-delighted with great pleasure, and such overwhelming pleasure cannot be comprehended by any individual except one who had such a situation befall him too! The individual can now go about his life, after expecting death. So he takes the reins of his riding beast exclaiming: "O Allah, You are my slave and I am your Lord!" So this individual intended to extol and praise Allah ﷺ and meant to say: "O Allah, You are my Lord and I am Your Servant!"

So this Hadith is a proof and evidence that Allah ﷺ becomes pleased with the repentance of His slave whenever he makes repentance to Him, and He the Exalted loves this greatly, but not for His Own self, no, but for the individual, as He the Exalted is free from want and need. This is merely out of love for His servant and out of His generosity. He the Exalted loves to forgive and overlook rather than take one to account for their wrongdoings, so this is the reason why He loves the repentant one.

So in this Hadith is an encouragement to the servant to repent for his wrongdoings, as Allah the Exalted loves and is pleased with this act, and it serves as a great benefit for that individual.

And also this Hadith contains a confirmation that Allah becomes delighted and pleased. And Allah can become pleased or angry and He dislikes and He loves; but in saying this, these attributes are not like those of Allah's creation, rather they are particular to Him only and Allah says regarding this in the Qur'an:

$$ لَيْسَ كَمِثْلِهِۦ شَيْءٌ وَهُوَ ٱلسَّمِيعُ ٱلْبَصِيرُ $$

"There is nothing like unto Him, and He is the All-Hearing, the All-Seer." (Ash-Shura 11)

So this delight Allah has, befits His Majesty, and is not likened to that of His creation.

And this Hadith also contains a proof that if the servant errs or makes a mistake in his (her) statement or action, even if that was committing or falling into an act of Kufr, that individual will not be held to account for that mistake. This is because this individual (in this Hadith) uttered a statement which is considered a clear act of Kufr, and that was when he said: "O Allah, You are my slave and I am Your Lord." This is clearly (a statement of) Kufr. And this is general, and also includes other similar statements; also, if an individual reviles another unintentionally without intending that or an individual divorces his wife, or frees his slave, without intending that matter, they will not be taken to account for them. All of these are equal to unintentional oaths and Allah ﷻ says:

30

لَا يُؤَاخِذُكُمُ ٱللَّهُ بِٱللَّغْوِ فِى أَيْمَـٰنِكُمْ وَلَـٰكِن يُؤَاخِذُكُم بِمَا كَسَبَتْ

قُلُوبُكُمْ ۗ وَٱللَّهُ غَفُورٌ حَلِيمٌ

"Allah will not call you to account for that which is unintentional in your oaths, but He will call you to account for what your hearts have earned." (Al-Baqarah, 225)

As for intentionally mocking (a Muslim or the Deen), belittling and idly joking, this is something different and it is outright disbelief; the one who mocks the Deen commits Kufr by such a deed as Allah says regarding this in the Qur'an:

وَلَئِن سَأَلْتَهُمْ لَيَقُولُنَّ إِنَّمَا كُنَّا نَخُوضُ وَنَلْعَبُ ۚ قُلْ أَبِٱللَّهِ

وَءَايَـٰتِهِۦ وَرَسُولِهِۦ كُنتُمْ تَسْتَهْزِءُونَ • لَا تَعْتَذِرُوا۟ قَدْ كَفَرْتُم

"If you ask them (about this), they declare: 'We were only talking idly and joking.' Say: 'Was it at Allah, His Ayaat (proofs, evidences, Verses, lessons, signs, revelations, etc.) and His Messenger that you were mocking?' Make no excuse; you have disbelieved." (At-Tawbah, 65-66)

So making mockery, ridiculing and making fun (of a Muslim, the Qur'an or anything from the Sunnah) intentionally is all tantamount to Kufr and the one who does this intentionally is a clear cut Kaafir, but if this was done unintentionally, this has a different ruling, and this is from the mercy of Allah. And Allah grants success!

[Hadith 16]

Abu Musa Al-Ash'ari ﷺ reported: The Messenger ﷺ said:

« إِنَّ اللهَ تعالى يَبْسُطُ يدَهُ بِاللَّيْلِ لِيَتُوبَ مُسيءُ النَّهَارِ وَيَبْسُطُ يدَهُ بِالنَّهَارِ لِيَتُوبَ مُسِيءُ اللَّيْلِ حَتَّى تَطْلُعَ الشَّمْسُ مِن مَغْرِبِهَا » رواه مسلم .

"Allah the Exalted, will continue to stretch out His Hand in the night so that the sinner of the day may repent, and continue to stretch out His Hand in the daytime so that the sinner of the night may repent, until the sun rises from the west." [Muslim]

[Hadith 17]

Abu Hurairah ﷺ narrated: Messenger of Allah ﷺ said:

« مَنْ تَابَ قَبْلَ أَنْ تَطْلُعَ الشَّمْسُ مِنْ مَغْرِبِهَا تَابَ اللهُ عَلَيْهِ » رواه مسلم .

"He who repents before the sun rises from the west, Allah will forgive him." [Muslim]

[Hadith 18]

Abdullah ibn Umar ibn Al-Khattaab ﷺ reported that the Prophet ﷺ said:

«إِنَّ اللهَ عَزَّ وَجَلَّ يَقْبَلُ تَوْبَةَ العَبْدِ مَالَمْ يُغَرْغِرْ» رواه الترمذي وقال: حديث حسنٌ .

"Allah accepts a slave's repentance as long as he is not on his death bed (that is, before the soul of the dying person reaches the throat)." [At-Tirmidhi]

[EXPLANATION OF HADITH 16 TO 18]

These three Hadiths are all related to repentance. As for the narration of Abu Musa Al-Ash'ari, it indicates Allah's great generosity, and that is in the fact that He even accepts the repentance of an individual who falls into wrongdoing, but delays repenting from that wrongdoing after some time has passed. So this means, if an individual commits a sin during the day and then seeks repentance during the night, Allah ﷻ accepts it. Likewise, if the slave commits a sin during the night, and seeks repentance during the day, Allah ﷻ accepts it; He stretches His Hand out to receive that repentance made by the believing slave.

This Hadith also contains a confirmation of the Hand of Allah, rather the Exalted has two Hands, and Allah makes this clear when He says in the Qur'an:

وَقَالَتِ ٱلۡيَهُودُ يَدُ ٱللَّهِ مَغۡلُولَةٌ ۚ غُلَّتۡ أَيۡدِيهِمۡ وَلُعِنُواْ بِمَا قَالُواْ ۘ بَلۡ يَدَاهُ مَبۡسُوطَتَانِ

"The Jews say: 'Allah's Hand is tied up (i.e. He does not give and spend of His Bounty).' Be their hands tied up and be accursed for what they uttered. Nay, both His Hands are widely outstretched." (Al-Maa'idah, 64)

So Allah the Exalted here confirms He has two Hands. Based upon this, it is binding upon us to have belief in them, as they are firmly established for Allah the Exalted. But in saying this, we say, it is impermissible for us to liken them to that of our hands as Allah says:

$$لَيْسَ كَمِثْلِهِۦ شَىْءٌ ۖ وَهُوَ ٱلسَّمِيعُ ٱلْبَصِيرُ$$

"There is nothing like unto Him, and He is the All-Hearer, All-Knowing." (Ash-Shura, 11)

Likewise, every time you come across an attribute of Allah as He confirms it, then know, that attribute is not similar to or like the attributes of His Creation, as nothing is like unto Him, nor His self, nor His description Exalted be He.

This Hadith also contains a proof that for sure Allah the Exalted accepts an individual's repentance, even if that individual delays it; in saying this, we must mention that it is an obligation upon every individual to hasten in seeking repentance, as one does not know when his life will suddenly be cut short, and it is possible that death could overtake that individual before they seek repentance from Allah. So it is obligatory to hasten it, but if it is delayed, Allah will still accept the servant's repentance.

The Hadith also proves that when the sun rises from the west, repentance will no longer be accepted. But if one was to ask: will the sun really rise from the west? As it is well known that it rises from the east? We reply to this by saying: Yes, this is true and yes, the sun does rise from the east, and this has been the case since the Exalted created it until now, but in the last days (before Judgement Day), Allah will command it to do the opposite, and that is to rise from it west. So when it does rise from the west, all will see it doing so and believe and affirm faith (in Allah being the only one worthy of worship) including the disbelievers, Jews, Christians, Buddhists, communists and other than them. All will attest faith in Allah alone. But this will not avail them in the least. And the narration of Abu Hurairah is similar to that of Abu Musa.

As for the narration of Ibn Umar ﷺ where the Prophet ﷺ said: "Allah accepts a slave's Repentance as long as he is not on his death bed (that is, before the soul of the dying person reaches the throat)", then this means Allah the Exalted will accept an individual's repentance as long as that individual makes it before their soul reaches the throat, but if it does reach that throat, then such a person's repentance will not be accepted by Allah, and this is established through other sources that such a repentance is outright rejected, such as the statement of Allah when He says:

$$\text{وَلَيْسَتِ ٱلتَّوْبَةُ لِلَّذِينَ يَعْمَلُونَ ٱلسَّيِّئَاتِ حَتَّىٰ إِذَا حَضَرَ أَحَدَهُمُ}$$

$$\text{ٱلْمَوْتُ قَالَ إِنِّي تُبْتُ ٱلْـَٰنَ}$$

"And of no effect is the repentance of those who continue to do evil deeds until death faces one of them and he says: 'Now I repent.'" (An-Nisaa', 18)

So Oh dear Muslim! Hasten, to repent to Allah for whatever wrongdoing you have committed or fallen into, and refrain from committing whatsoever sin you are indulging in! Make speedy effort in practising that which is mandated upon you from Allah's commandments. We ask the Exalted and High to accept out repentance and for sure Allah grants success!

Zir ibn Hubaish reported:

أَتَيْتُ صَفْوَانَ بْنِ عَسَّالٍ رضي الله عنه أَسْأَلُهُ عن الْمَسْحِ عَلَى الْخُفَّيْنِ فقال : مَا جَاءَبِكَ يَا زُرُّ؟ فَقُلْتُ : ابْتِغَاءُ الْعِلْمِ، فقال: إِنَّ الْمَلَائِكَةَ تَضَعُ أَجْنِحتِها لِطَالِبِ الْعِلْمِ رِضاء بِمَا يَطْلُبُ، فَقُلْتُ: إِنَّه قَدْ حَكَّ في صَدْرِي الْمَسْحُ عَلَى الْخُفَّيْنِ بَعْدَ الْغَائِطِ والْبَوْلِ، وكُنْتَ امْرَءاً مِنْ أَصْحاب النَّبِيِّ ﷺ، فَجِئْتُ أَسْأَلُكَ: هَلْ سَمِعْتَهُ يَذْكُرُ في ذَلِكَ شيئاً ؟ قال : نعَمْ كانَ يأْمُرنا إذا كُنا سفَراً أَوْ مُسافِرين أَنْ لا نَنْزِعَ خِفافَنا ثلاثة أَيَّام وَلَياليهِنَّ إِلَّا مِنْ جنابةٍ، لكِنْ مِنْ غائِطٍ وبَوْلٍ ونَوْم. فقُلْتُ: هَل سَمِعتهُ يذْكر في الهَوى شيئاً؟ قال: نعم كُنَّا مَع رسول الله ﷺ في سفرٍ، فبيْنا نحنُ عِنْدهُ إذ نادَاهُ أَعْرابي بصوْتٍ له جهوريٍّ: يا مُحمَّدُ ، فأَجابهُ رسولُ الله ﷺ نحْوا مِنْ صَوْتِه: «هَاؤُمْ» فقُلْتُ لهُ: وَيْحَكَ اغْضُضْ مِنْ صَوْتِكَ فإِنَّك عِند النَّبِيِّ ﷺ وقد نُهِيت عَنْ هذا، فقال: والله لا أَغضُضُ. قَالَ الأَعْرابِيُّ: الْمَرْءُ يُحِبُّ الْقَوم ولَمَّا يلْحق بِهِمْ؟ قال النَّبِيُّ ﷺ: «الْمَرْءُ مع مِنْ أَحَبَّ يَوْمَ الْقِيامِةِ » فما زَالَ يُحَدِّثُنا حتَّى ذكَر باباً مِن الْمَغْرِب مَسيرَةُ عَرْضِه أَوْ يَسِير الرَّاكِبُ في عَرْضِه أَرْبَعِينَ أَوْ سَبْعِينَ عَاماً. قَالَ سُفْيَانُ أَحدُ الرُّوَاة. قِبل الشَّام خلقُهُ الله تعالى يوْم خلق السموات والأَرْضَ مَفْتوحاً لِلتَّوبةِ لا يُغلَقُ حتَّى تَطلُعَ الشَّمْسُ مِنْهُ» رواه التِّرمذي وغيره وقال: حديث حسن صحيح

"I went to Safwaan ibn Assaal to inquire about wiping with wet hands over the khuffs (socks) while performing Wudu. He asked me: 'What brings you here, Zir?' I answered: 'The desire for knowledge.' He said: 'Angels spread their wings for the seeker of knowlege out of joy for what he seeks.' I told him: 'I have some doubts in my mind regarding wiping of wet hands over the khuffs in the course of performing Wudu after defecation or urinating. Now since you are one of the Companions of the Prophet ﷺ, I have come to ask you whether you heard any saying of the Prophet concerning it?' He replied in the affirmative and said: 'He instructed us that during a journey we need not take *off our khuffs for washing the feet up to three days and nights, except in the case of major impurity (after sexual intercourse). In other cases such as sleeping, relieving oneself or urinating, the wiping of wet hands over khuffs will suffice.' I then, questioned him, 'Did you hear him say anything about love and affection?' He replied: 'We accompanied the Messenger of Allah ﷺ in a journey when a bedouin called out in a loud voice, "O Muhammad." The Messenger of Allah replied him in the same tone: "Here I am." I said to him (the bedouin): "Woe to you, lower your voice in His presentence, because you are not allowed to do so." He said: "By Allah! I will not lower my voice," and then addressing the Prophet ﷺ he said: "What about a person who loves a people but has not found himself in their company?" The Messenger of Allah ﷺ replied: "On the Day of Resurrection, a person will be in the company with those whom he loves." The Messenger of Allah ﷺ then kept on talking to us and in the course of his talk, he mentioned a gateway in the heaven, the width of which could be crossed by a rider in forty or seventy years.'"*

Sufyaan, one of the narrators of this tradition, said: "This gateway is in the direction of Syria. Allah created it on the day He created the heavens and the earth. It is open for repentance and will not be shut until the sun rises from that direction (i.e., the west)." [At-Tirmidhi]

[EXPLANATION OF HADITH 19]

The author (Imam An-Nawawi) mentions this narration to clarify when repentance will be discontinued. So this narration has the following benefits that can be derived from it, including:

Zir ibn Hubaish went to Safwaan ibn Assaal in search of knowledge of the Deen, meaning knowledge of what Prophet Muhammad ﷺ brought, but as for knowledge regarding worldly matters, then they are sought for worldly reasons, but as for seeking knowledge (Ilm), it is that which Prophet Muhammad ﷺ brought. This is what the Qur'an and Sunnah encourages and praises those who go in search of it or possess it, and seeking it is considered a type of Jihaad for the sake of Allah, as for sure this is one of the two matters which the Deen is built upon:

- Knowledge and clarification.
- (Jihaad) by weapons, swords and spears.

Some of the scholars have even said: Seeking Ilm is more virtuous than performing Jihaad in the cause of Allah. This is because safeguarding the religion is surely done by knowledge and Jihaad by the sword can only be fought based upon knowledge as it is not possible for the Mujaahid to fight, subdue, divide the war booty or treat prisoners correctly except by way of knowledge, and for this reason Allah the Exalted says in the Qur'an:

يَرْفَعِ ٱللَّهُ ٱلَّذِينَ ءَامَنُوا۟ مِنكُمْ وَٱلَّذِينَ أُوتُوا۟ ٱلْعِلْمَ دَرَجَٰتٍ

"Allah will exalt in degree those of you who believe, and those who have been granted knowledge." (Al-Mujaadilah, 11)

So regarding Safwaan's words in this narration: "Angels spread their wings for the seeker of knowledge out of joy for what he seeks", the angels do this out respect and honour for that individual, due to them seeking knowledge.

If it is said: I cannot perceive this? That is, the angels spreading their wings for the seeker of knowledge out of joy for what he seeks, we say: if this information is affirmed (and it is) from the Prophet ﷺ, then belief in it is binding upon the believer. And this is similar to the Prophet's ﷺ statement:

إنَّ اللهَ يَنْزِلُ إلى السَّماء الدُّنيا حِينَ يَبْقَ ثُلُثُ اللَّيل الآخِر فَيَقُولُ: مَنْ يَدْعُوني فَأَسْتَجِيبُ لهُ ,

مَنْ يَسْأَلُني فَأَعْطِيهِ ,مَنْ يَسْتَغْفِرُني فَأَغْفِرُ لهُ

"Every night when it is the last third of the night, our Lord descends to the nearest heavens and says; 'Is there anyone to invoke Me that I may respond to his invocation? Is there anyone to ask Me so that I may grant him his request? Is there anyone asking My forgiveness so that I forgive him?'"

So it was not actually us that received this narration directly, rather, the Prophet ﷺ did from Allah the Exalted, but like we have said elsewhere, if the Prophet ﷺ received information regarding a matter, it is tantamount to us also hearing this information. So it is an obligation upon us to have sure belief in whatever is confirmed from the Prophet ﷺ regarding matters related to the unseen, and we have to perceive such information as though we witnessed this with our very eyes, whatever the matter may be. So regarding the rest of this narration, then Zir ibn Hubaish said to Safwaan ibn Assaal, he had reservations regarding wiping wet hands over the *khuffs* (or leather socks) after relieving oneself, so regarding this Allah the Exalted says in the Qur'an:

$$\text{يَـٰٓأَيُّهَا ٱلَّذِينَ ءَامَنُوٓاْ إِذَا قُمْتُمْ إِلَى ٱلصَّلَوٰةِ فَٱغْسِلُواْ وُجُوهَكُمْ}$$

$$\text{وَأَيْدِيَكُمْ إِلَى ٱلْمَرَافِقِ وَٱمْسَحُواْ بِرُءُوسِكُمْ وَأَرْجُلَكُمْ إِلَى ٱلْكَعْبَيْنِ}$$

"O you who believe! When you intend to offer prayer, wash your faces and your hands (fore-arms) up to the elbows, rub (by passing wet hands over) your heads, and (wash) your feet up to ankles." (Al-Maa'idah, 6)

So regarding Zir's statement in this narration when he said: "I have some doubts in my mind" This means, he was confused and doubtful regarding wiping over *khuffs* after relieving himself: is wiping over the *khuffs* (or socks) allowed or not? So, Safwaan ibn Assaal clarified the matter, that it is allowed, because the Prophet ﷺ gave them the concession to do so and informed them that whenever travelling, they were allowed to wipe over them except while in the state of major impurity, but as for relieving themselves and sleep, them wiping them was allowed.

And it is confirmed in Al-Bukhari and Muslim that Al-Mughirah ibn Shu'bah was with the Prophet ﷺ on one of his journeys so the Prophet ﷺ went to perform Wudu, so Al-Mughirah went to take off the Prophet's *khuffs* so the Prophet ﷺ said to him:

$$\text{دَعْهُمَا فَإِنِّي أَدْخَلْتُهُمَا طَاهِرَتَيْنِ}$$

"Leave them for I had put them on after performing ablution."

This Hadith is a clear proof indicating the preference of wiping over whatsoever is on the feet rather than removing that which is upon one's feet.

Also from the benefits of this Hadith: that it is a must upon an individual if any matter regarding the Deen becomes confusing or doubtful to them to go to those with knowledge, so as to clarify that matter to them; this is because there are many individuals who have doubts within themselves and are very confused regarding Deen-related matters and for some reason or the other they do not go to get to those with knowledge to get those matters clarified, so they remain in a utterly bewildered state and confused, and this is a big mistake. To avoid being bewildered, confused and doubtful within one's self, one should, like this Hadith indicates, ask those with knowledge so as to have a sound state of mind. This narration clearly points to this. Zir went out to Safwaan ibn Assaal asking him regarding wiping over the *khuffs*, and if he had heard anything regarding this from the Prophet ﷺ, to which he replied:

كانَ يَأْمُرنا إذا كُنَّا سفراً أوْ مُسافِرِين أَن لا نَنْزِعَ خِفافَنا ثلاثة أَيَّام ولَيَاليهنَّ إلاَّ مِنْ جَنابةٍ ، لكِنْ
مِنْ غائطٍ وبَوْلٍ ونَوْمٍ

"He instructed us that during a journey we need not take off our khuffs for washing the feet up to three days and nights, except in the case in major impurity (after sexual intercourse). In other cases such as sleeping, relieving oneself or urinating, the wiping of wet hands over khuffs will suffice."

In this narration is a confirmation of the permissibility of wiping over whatsoever is one's feet, and regarding this issue the narrations are *Mutawaatir* (reported by a large number of narrators whose agreement on a lie is inconceivable, on all levels of the chain of narration from the beginning to the end), and to indicate its lofty status, even those who have written books of Aqeedah, have even mentioned the wiping over *khuffs* in their books and one of the reasons for this is due to the fact that the Raafidah-Shia reject it and say it is not allowed and nothing is confirmed regarding it.

But we say: how strange their views are! Believe it or not, one of those who narrate wiping of the *khuffs* is none other than Ali ibn Abi Taalib ☺! But with great regret they still deny it. So we say: the wiping over whatsoever is on the feet is a great slogan and from the rituals of the people of the Sunnah which is *Mutawaatir* from the Prophet ☺, without doubt. And for this reason Imam Ahmed said: "There is not a shadow of doubt in my mind concerning the legality of wiping over the leather socks." And he said: "There are forty narrations of the Prophet ☺ and his companions indicating its permissibility."

Zir further inquired: "Did you hear him say anything about love and affection?" So Safwaan mentioned to Zir the story of a bedouin approaching the Prophet ☺ saying: "O Muhammad!" Safwaan ibn Assal then said to this bedouin: "Woe to you, lower your voice in his presence." This was told to the bedouin due to the statement of Allah the Exalted when He says in the Qur'an:

يَـٰٓأَيُّهَا ٱلَّذِينَ ءَامَنُواْ لَا تَرْفَعُوٓاْ أَصْوَٰتَكُمْ فَوْقَ صَوْتِ ٱلنَّبِيِّ وَلَا تَجْهَرُواْ لَهُۥ بِٱلْقَوْلِ كَجَهْرِ بَعْضِكُمْ لِبَعْضٍ أَن تَحْبَطَ أَعْمَٰلُكُمْ وَأَنتُمْ لَا تَشْعُرُونَ

"O you who believe! Raise not your voices above the voice of the Prophet, nor speak aloud to Him in talk as you speak aloud to one another, lest your deeds may be rendered fruitless while you perceive not." (Al-Hujuraat, 2)

Regarding the bedouins, one of the reasons why they would behave this way, with a lack of respect and manners, was due to the fact that they did not used to live in the city, but far from it, and also, they had little knowledge regarding the Deen, and were far from the circles of knowledge. When this bedouin addressed that Prophet ﷺ in this manner, the Prophet ﷺ similarly addressed him in the same fashion. The Prophet ﷺ was the most complete individual in guidance and he would treat each individual according to the way that person was accustomed to and according to that person's level of understanding, so how people dealt with the Prophet, he too would deal with them accordingly. So this bedouin said: "What about a person who loves a people but has not found himself in their company?" Meaning, an individual loves a certain group of individuals but, his actions are not equal to theirs nor are his deeds on the same footing or comparison to that of theirs. So will such individual be with them or not? So the Prophet ﷺ replied by saying: "On the Day of Resurrection, a person will be in the company with those whom he loves."

So *Al-Hamdu lillah*! This is surely a great blessing indeed, and a similar portion of this narration is also narrated by Anas bin Maalik, wherein the Prophet ﷺ said: "Verily, you will be with those you love." So upon hearing this Anas said: "I dearly love the Messenger of Allah and Abu Bakr as well as Umar and I will be raised with them."

And we also bear witness that Allah alone deserves to be worshipped and we too dearly love the Messenger ﷺ and the Rightly Guided Caliphs as well as the rest of the Companions of the Prophet and the noble Imams after them, so we ask Allah the Exalted to raise us with them of the Day of Judgement!

This is a clear glad-tiding for the Muslim, that if he loves a certain group of people he will be with them on the Day of Resurrection and he too will be with them when they drink from the Pond of the Prophet ﷺ. So it becomes a must upon the Muslims to dislike the disbelievers, and to know that they are his enemies, no matter what bond there is between you and them, because one has to remember, the Kaafir only befriends one due to some personal benefit, and that is for himself, or it is to bring upon you some harm. And it is very unlikely that he befriends you for your own personal benefit, no, so how is it possible that your enemy brings benefit to your life, while at the same time his objective is to ruin and destroy you!? That is like trying to combine fire and water together. Is this possible!? So how can one expect the Kaafir to like or love you, while at the same time he is your open enemy whose objective is to bring about your destruction! So regarding this Allah ﷻ Himself calls them His enemies as well as our enemies when He says in the Qur'an:

يَـٰٓأَيُّهَا ٱلَّذِينَ ءَامَنُوا۟ لَا تَتَّخِذُوا۟ عَدُوِّى وَعَدُوَّكُمْ أَوْلِيَآءَ

"O you who believe! Take not My enemies and your enemies (disbelievers and polytheist) as friends." (Al-Mumtahinah, 1)

Also He says:

مَن كَانَ عَدُوًّا لِّلَّهِ وَمَلَـٰٓئِكَتِهِۦ وَرُسُلِهِۦ وَجِبْرِيلَ وَمِيكَىٰلَ فَإِنَّ ٱللَّهَ

عَدُوٌّ لِّلْكَـٰفِرِينَ

"Whosoever is an enemy to Allah, His Angels, His Messengers, Gabriel and Michael, then verily, Allah is an enemy to the disbelievers." (Al-Baqarah, 98)

So based upon this, Allah is an enemy to every disbeliever, and every disbeliever is also our enemy; they bring nothing to us accept evil. It is biding upon you to dislike them in your heart, whosoever they may be or whatever close bond they have to you! So know, for sure he is your open enemy, as we cited to you the statement of Allah when He says: **"O you who believe! Take not My enemies and your enemies (disbelievers and polytheist) as friends."** So again, "A person will be in the company with those whom he loves." So increase your devotion and love for Allah and His Messenger ﷺ, his notable Companions and the Imams of guidance and those after them. We ask Allah the Exalted to make that a sure reality and for sure Allah grants success.

[Hadith 20]

Abu Sa'id Al-Khudri reported: The Prophet of Allah ﷺ said:

« كانَ فِيمَنْ كانَ قَبْلَكُمْ رَجُلٌ قتَل تِسْعةً وتِسْعينَ نفْساً، فسألَ عن أعلَمِ أَهْلِ الأرْضِ فدُلَّ على راهِبٍ، فأتَاهُ فقال: إنَّهُ قَتَل تِسعةً وتِسعينَ نَفْساً، فَهلْ لَهُ مِنْ تَوْبَةٍ ؟ فقال: لا فقتلَهُ فكمَّلَ بِهِ مِائَةً ثُمَّ سألَ عن أعلمِ أهلِ الأرضِ، فدُلَّ على رجلٍ عالِمٍ فقال: إنَه قَتَل مِائة نفسٍ فهلْ لَهُ مِنْ تَوْبَةٍ؟ فقالَ: نَعَمْ ومنْ يَحُولُ بَيْنَهُ وبَيْنَ التوْبةِ؟ انطَلِقْ إلَى أرْضِ كذا وكذا، فإنَّ بِها أُناساً يعْبُدُونَ الله تعالى فاعْبُدِ اللهَ مَعَهُمْ، ولا تَرْجِعْ إلى أرْضِكَ فإنَّها أرْضُ سُوءٍ، فانطَلَق حتَّى إذا نَصَف الطَّرِيقُ أتَاهُ الموْتُ فاخْتصمتْ فِيهِ مَلائكةُ الرَّحمَةِ ومَلائكةُ العَذابِ. فقالتْ ملائكةُ الرَّحمَةِ: جاءَ تائِباً مُقْبِلا بِقلْبِهِ إلى اللهِ تعالى، وقالتْ ملائكةُ العذابِ: إنَّهُ لمْ يَعْمَلْ خيْراً قطُّ، فأتَاهُمْ مَلكٌ في صُورَةِ آدمي فجعلوهُ بيْنهُمْ أي حكماً فقال قيسوا ما بَيْنَ الأرْضَيْنِ فإلى أيَّتِهما كان أدْنى فهو لَهُ، فقاسُوا فوَجدُوه أدْنى إلى الأرْضِ التي أرَادَ فقبَضتْهُ مَلائكةُ الرَّحمةِ » متفقٌ عليه.

وفي روايةٍ في الصحِيحِ : « فكانَ إلَى القَرْيَةِ الصَّالِحَةِ أقْرَب بِشِبْرٍ ، فجُعِل مِنْ أهْلِها » وفي روايةٍ في الصحيحِ: « فأوْحَى اللهُ تعالى إلَى هذِهِ أَنْ تَبَاعَدِي، وإلى هذهِ أَنْ تَقَرَّبِي وقَال: قِيسُوا مَا بينهُما ، فوَجدُوه إلى هذِهِ أقْرَب بِشِبْرٍ فغُفِرَ لَهُ ». وفي روايةٍ : « فنأى بِصَدْرِه نَحْوَها ».

"There was a man from among a nation before you who killed 99 people and then made an inquiry about the most learned person on the earth. He was directed to a monk. He came to him and told him that he had killed 99 people and asked him if there was any chance for his repentance to be accepted. The monk replied in the negative and the man killed him completing 100. He then asked about the most learned man in the earth. He was directed to a scholar. He told him that he had killed 100 people and if there was any chance of this repentance being accepted. He replied in the affirmative and asked: 'Who stands between you and repentance?

Go to such- and-such land; there (you will find) people devoted to prayer and worship of Allah, join them in worship, and do not come back to your land as it is an evil place.' So he went away and hardly had he covered half the distance when death overtook him; and there was a dispute between the angels of mercy and the angels of torment. The angels of mercy pleaded. 'This man has come with a repentant heart to Allah,' and the angels of punishment argued, 'He had never done a virtuous deed in his life!' Then there appeared another angel in the form of a human being and the contending angels agreed to make him arbitrate between them. He said: 'Measure the distance of the two lands. He will be considered to belong to the land to which he is nearest.' They measured it and found him closer to the land (land of piety) where he intended to go, and so the angels of mercy collected his soul." [Agreed Upon]

In another narration in the Sahih: "He was found to be nearer to the locality of the pious by a cubit and was thus included among them."

Another version in the Sahih says: "Allah commanded (the land which he wanted to leave) to move away and commanded the other land (his destination) to draw nearer and then He said: 'Now measure the distance between them.'" It was found that he was nearer to his goal by a hand's span and was thus forgiven." It is also narrated that he drew closer by a slight movement of his chest.

[EXPLANATION OF HADITH 20]

So the author (Imam An-Nawawi) mentions this narration narrated by Sa'id Al-Khudri wherein the Prophet ﷺ said: "There was a man from among a nation before you who killed 99 people." This individual felt deep remorse over what he had done so he asked for the most learned individual on the earth to inquire whether or not his repentance would be accepted, and he was directed to this monk, who it was said, was a devout worshipper, but ignorant, without knowledge. The man informed the monk that he had killed 99 people and asked whether his repentance would be accepted or not? This monk considered what he had done to be too great to be forgiven, and he informed him: "Your repentance will not be accepted." So the man become extremely annoyed and angry and killed the monk making it 100 murders.

Then the man asked where he could find the most learned individual on the earth and so he was guided to a Scholar, so he informed him that he had killed 100 people, and asked if is repentance would be accepted? So the Scholar replied to him saying, "Yes, what can prevent you from that?" – meaning: the door of repentance was open. So the Scholar advised the man to go to such-and-such land wherein those people worshipped Allah ﷻ.

Allah knows best, but it seems that the land he was in was a country of disbelievers. The Scholar told the man to make Hijrah (migration) to this new location, and so the man left, remorseful, repentant and a migrant, to this new land wherein they worshipped Allah alone. But along the path death overtook him and the angels of mercy and angels of torment disputed over him; the angels of torment, and we seek Allah's refuge, take the soul of the disbeliever while the angels of mercy take the Muslim souls.

The angels of torment argued that the man had not done an atom's weight of good ever, meaning: after he made repentance, whereas the angels of mercy argued the opposite and said he had made repentance and was remorseful, so they differed over the matter until Allah sent an angel to judge in their affair. So he said measure between both lands and whichever land the man was closest to then he is from those people. And since he was closer to the land of Emaan, the angel of mercy took his soul.

This hadith has many benefits including:

The murderer's repentance is accepted and this is backed by the Exalted's statement in the Qur'an:

إِنَّ ٱللَّهَ لَا يَغْفِرُ أَن يُشْرَكَ بِهِۦ وَيَغْفِرُ مَا دُونَ ذَٰلِكَ لِمَن يَشَآءُ

"Verily, Allah forgives not that partners should be set up with Him in worship, but He forgives except that (anything else) to whom He pleases." (An-Nisaa', 48)

Meaning: He forgives all sins except *Shirk* if He pleases. And this is a collective view of the scholars on this matter. It is narrated that Abdullah ibn Abbas ﷺ said: **"The murderer's repentance is not accepted."** And he said this due to the statement of Allah:

وَمَن يَقْتُلْ مُؤْمِنًا مُّتَعَمِّدًا فَجَزَآؤُهُۥ جَهَنَّمُ خَٰلِدًا فِيهَا وَغَضِبَ ٱللَّهُ

عَلَيْهِ وَلَعَنَهُۥ وَأَعَدَّ لَهُۥ عَذَابًا عَظِيمًا

"And whoever kills a believer intentionally, his (her) recompense is Hell to abide therein, and the Wrath and the Curse of Allah and upon him (her), and a great punishment is prepared from him (her)." (An-Nisaa', 93)

But that which is the collective view of the scholars is the most correct view and opinion on this matter. And regarding Ibn Abbas's view, it is possible that what he meant was: the murdered might not forgive the murderer. And three have rights over the murderer: Allah, the murdered and the guardians of the murdered.

As for Allah's rights, no doubt Allah the Exalted accepts the murderer's repentance if he repents and this is due to His statement in the Qur'an when He says:

قُلْ يَـٰعِبَادِىَ ٱلَّذِينَ أَسْرَفُوا۟ عَلَىٰٓ أَنفُسِهِمْ لَا تَقْنَطُوا۟ مِن رَّحْمَةِ ٱللَّهِ ۚ إِنَّ

ٱللَّهَ يَغْفِرُ ٱلذُّنُوبَ جَمِيعًا ۚ إِنَّهُۥ هُوَ ٱلْغَفُورُ ٱلرَّحِيمُ

"Say: "My slaves who have transgressed against themselves (by committing evil deeds and sins)! Despair not of the Mercy of Allah, verily Allah forgives all sins."" (Az-Zumar, 53)

Allah also says:

وَٱلَّذِينَ لَا يَدْعُونَ مَعَ ٱللَّهِ إِلَـٰهًا ءَاخَرَ وَلَا يَقْتُلُونَ ٱلنَّفْسَ ٱلَّتِى

حَرَّمَ ٱللَّهُ إِلَّا بِٱلْحَقِّ وَلَا يَزْنُونَ ۚ وَمَن يَفْعَلْ ذَٰلِكَ يَلْقَ أَثَامًا •

يُضَـٰعَفْ لَهُ ٱلْعَذَابُ يَوْمَ ٱلْقِيَـٰمَةِ وَيَخْلُدْ فِيهِۦ مُهَانًا • إِلَّا مَن تَابَ

وَءَامَنَ وَعَمِلَ عَمَلًا صَلِحًا فَأُوْلَـٰٓئِكَ يُبَدِّلُ ٱللَّهُ سَيِّـَٔاتِهِمْ حَسَنَـٰتٍ وَكَانَ ٱللَّهُ غَفُورًا رَّحِيمًا

"And those who invoke not any other ilah (god) along with Allah, nor kill such life as Allah has forbidden, except for a just cause, nor commit illegal sexual intercourse; and whoever does this shall receive the punishment. The torment will be doubled to him on the Day of Resurrection, and he will abide therein in disgrace, except those who repent and believe (in Islamic Monotheism), and do righteous deeds; for those, Allah will change their sins into good deeds, and Allah is Oft-Forgiving, Most Merciful." (Al-Furqaan, 68-70)

As for the murdered victim's right, the murderer's repenting for what he has done will be of no use to him, and he will give the murdered victim's right back to him (for killing him) on the Day of Judgement, and Allah the Exalted will decide their matter and judge between them.

As for the right of the guardians: then the murderer will bear a heavy burden until he confesses what he has done to the murdered victim's guardians and gives himself up to them saying: "I am the one guilty of the murder! Either ordain the prescribed punishment for murder upon me, or take what is due from me, or overlook my error by forgiving me."

[Hadith 22]

Imraan ibn Hussain Al-Khuza'i reported:

وَعَنْ أَبِي نُجَيْد بِضَمِّ النُّونِ وَفَتْحِ الْجِيمِ عِمْرَانَ بْنِ الْحُصَيْنِ الْخُزَاعِيّ رَضِيَ اللهُ عَنْهُمَا أَنَّ امْرَأَةً مِنْ جُهَيْنَةَ
أَتَتْ رَسُولَ اللهِ ﷺ وَهِيَ حُبْلَى مِنَ الزِّنَا، فَقَالَتْ: يَا رَسُولَ اللهِ أَصَبْتُ حَدًّا فَأَقِمْهُ عَلَيَّ، فَدَعَا نَبِيُّ اللهِ ﷺ
وَلِيَّهَا فَقَالَ: أَحْسِنْ إِلَيْهَا، فَإِذَا وَضَعَتْ فَأْتِنِي فَفَعَلَ فَأَمَرَ بِهَا نَبِيُّ اللهِ ﷺ، فَشُدَّتْ عَلَيْهَا ثِيَابُهَا، ثُمَّ أَمَرَ
بِهَا فَرُجِمَتْ، ثُمَّ صَلَّى عَلَيْهَا. فَقَالَ لَهُ عُمَرُ: تُصَلِّي عَلَيْهَا يَا رَسُولَ اللهِ وَقَدْ زَنَتْ، قَالَ: لَقَدْ تَابَتْ تَوْبَةً
لَوْ قُسِمَتْ بَيْنَ سَبْعِينَ مِنْ أَهْلِ الْمَدِينَةِ لَوَسِعَتْهُمْ وَهَلْ وَجَدْتَ أَفْضَلَ مِنْ أَنْ جَادَتْ بِنَفْسِهَا لِلَّهِ عَزَّ
وَجَلَّ» رَوَاهُ مُسْلِم.

A woman from the tribe of Juhainah came to the Messenger of Allah ﷺ while she was pregnant from Zina (adultery) and said to Him: "O Messenger of Allah! I have committed an offence liable to Hadd (prescribed punishment), so exact the execution of the sentence. The Messenger of Allah ﷺ called for her guardian and said to him: "Treat her kindly. Bring her to me after the delivery of the child." That man complied with the orders. At last the Prophet ﷺ commanded to carry out the sentence. Her clothes were secured around her and she was stoned to death. The Prophet ﷺ led her funeral prayers. Umar submitted: "O Messenger of Allah! She committed Zina and you have performed funeral prayers for her? He replied: "Verily, she made repentance which would suffice for 70 of the people of Al-Madinah if it was divided among them. Can there be any higher degree of repentance than that she sacrificed her life voluntarily to win the pleasure of Allah, the Exalted?" [Muslim]

[EXPLANATION OF HADITH 22]

The author (Imam An-Nawawi) ﷺ mentions the narration of
Imraan ibn Hussain Al-Khuza'i where a woman came to the
Prophet ﷺ and as the narration says: "She was pregnant from
Zina (adultery)." This means that she became pregnant as a
result of committing Zina. She said: "O Messenger of Allah! I
have committed an offence liable to the *Hadd* (prescribed
punishment), so exact the execution of the sentence."
Meaning, I have committed an act that entails the ordained
punishment being implemented upon me. So the Prophet ﷺ
called for her guardian and told him to be good towards her
till she gives birth and once she did that, she should be
brought to the Prophet ﷺ; when she gave birth, her guardian
came to the Prophet ﷺ with her then "at last the Prophet
commanded to carry out the sentence and her clothes were
secured around her." This means to tie and bound a rope
around her so as to avoid her becoming uncovered or exposed
in front of all the people; then "(the Prophet ﷺ commanded
that) she be stoned to death." This means using stones or rocks
which are neither too big nor too small. So she was stoned till
she died. Then he ﷺ prayed over her and made Dua for her so
Umar said: "O Messenger of Allah! She committed Zina and
You have performed funeral prayers for her?" Meaning: isn't
Zina counted as a major sin? So the Prophet ﷺ replied:
"Verily, she made repentance which would suffice for 70 of
the people of Al-Madinah if it was divided among them." So
this means, if her repentance was divided among seventy
wrong doers from Al-Madinah, this would benefit them
greatly.

"Can there be any higher degree of repentance than that she sacrificed her life voluntarily to win the pleasure of Allah, the Exalted?" i.e. is there a better standing an individual can have (with Allah), then such a woman who, on her own accord, sacrificed her life! She handed herself over to the Prophet ﷺ merely based upon her deep level of God-consciousness of the Exalted. And she did this to also set herself free from the wrongdoing of Zina. So what could be done more better than this?

This hadith has many benefits including:

A clear indication that if an individual commits Zina and he is married then it is obligatory that such individual be stoned to death, and this ruling is backed up by the Qur'an. It was known that the Prophet ﷺ (commanded) stoning in his time as well as his Companions after him. And this ruling used to be in the Qur'an (stoning the adulators) but Allah, due to His Wisdom, later ordered that it be removed from the Qur'an literally, but the ruling still remained; that is, the ruling should still be implemented and put into practise.

So the married individual's punishment for Zina is stoning to death, and that is by putting this individual in a wide open space with people gathered to witness, then this individual is stoned till they die. And for sure this prescribed way of punishment is a clear indication of Allah's great wisdom, as the Deen did not order the way to execute the one who commits Zina to be struck by the sword, no, as this would be a very fast way to kill someone; rather, the Deen chose to make it be done by using stones. Why? To make the individual taste his bitter punishment for committing Zina. So the whole body most suffer pain similar to when the act of Zina was committed, when the whole body enjoyed the act of pleasure.

The scholars have said (regarding the type of stones used): It is impermissible to use very big stones! The reason being, the individual will avoid feeling pain, and the matter will be over quickly and he will die automatically. And the same goes for using little stones, this will be too agonizing and painful and the individual's death will be overly prolonged. Rather medium moderate size stones suffice, so that the individual feels severe pain up until his (or her) death.

So if it was said: is it not so, that the Prophet ﷺ said:

فَإِذَا قَتَلْتُم فَأَحْسِنُوا الْقِتْلَةَ وَإِذَا ذَبَحْتُم فَأَحْسِنُوا الذِّبْحَة

"So when you kill, you must make the killing in the best manner; when you slaughter, make your slaughter in the best manner."

And is not the sword more preferred, quicker and less agonising then stoning the person to death? We say: yes it is! But the best and most suitable manner of killing is what the Religion endorses as well as what agrees with it. And stoning is what the Deen considers the most suitable and best manner. Say a wrong doer intentionally killed another individual and before he killed him he beat him, similar we first will beat him then after that we will then kill him. For example: say a transgressing individual kills a particular person by cutting of his hands, then his feet, then his tongue and then his head, we will not kill this individual by simply killing him with a sword. No! Rather we will first cut off his hands, then feet, then tongue, then head, just as they did to the victim. And this is deemed the best and most suitable manner which is in accordance with the Deen.

In this hadith is also a proof for the following: the permissibility of confessing to committing Zina, and this not done merely so that this individual exposes himself, no, rather this is done as a means to purify himself from that act through the prescribed punishment. So one is not blamed nor reproached if one hands himself over to those in authority and the likes, to administer the prescribed punishment upon him.

As for exposing oneself to others in general, like informing the common folk that he has committed Zina which serves no purpose, then this is completely Haraam and one is exposing himself to the threat of not being forgiven for that sin as the Prophet ﷺ said in a narration:

كُلُّ أُمَّتِي مُعَافًى إِلَّا الْمُجَاهِرِينَ، قَالُوا مَن الْمُجَاهِرُون؟ الَّذِي يَفْعَل الذَّنب ثُمَّ سَتَرَهُ اللهُ عَلَيْهِ ثُمَّ يُصْبِحَ يَتَحَدث بِه

"'Every one of my followers will be forgiven except those who expose (openly) their wrongdoings.' So [the companions] said: 'Who are those who expose their sins?' [He replied:] 'An example of this is that of a man who commits a sin which Allah covers for him and in the morning, he says (to people): 'I committed such-and-such sin.'"

The other type of individual is the one who is a disobedient sinful bragger, who openly brags about committing Zina, as if this is something to feel proud about, and we seek Allah's refuge from this! So he says words like, "I travelled to so-and-so country, and committed Zina with such-and-such amount of women." Such an individual is requested to repent and if he does not, then he should be killed (by the authorities), as such a person who boasts about committing Zina, and considers it lawful is a disbeliever and this also includes other major sins one deems lawful.

If it is said: would it be better if one who fell into committing Zina hand himself in to a judge and confess to doing that, or would it be deemed better not to do that and to conceal committing Zina?

The matter needs to be explained and further elaboration is needed:

If the individual commits such acts like Zina, and then he sincerely repents to Allah feeling remorseful about falling into that, knowing he will not commit that act again, then in this case it would be better to conceal the act, and not to inform the judge; rather such individuals should keep that matter secret between them and Allah. As for if he knows he will continue committing Zina and not make sincere repentance from this, then in this case, it would be in his favour and best interest, rather than continuing to commit Zina, to hand himself in so as to be executed according to the prescribe l punishment for Zina.

[Hadith 23]

Ibn Abbas and Anas bin Maalik ﷺ reported: Messenger of Allah ﷺ said:

« لَوْ أَنَّ لِابْنِ آدَمَ وَادِياً مِنْ ذَهَبٍ أَحَبَّ أَنْ يَكُونَ لَهُ وَادِيانِ ، وَلَنْ يَمْلَأَ فَاهُ إِلَّا التُّرَابُ ، وَيَتُوبُ اللهُ عَلَى مَنْ تَابَ » مُتَّفَقٌ عَلَيْهِ .

"If a son of Adam were to own a valley full of gold, he would desire to have two. Nothing can fill his mouth except the earth (of his grave). Allah turns with mercy to him who turns to Him in repentance." [Agreed Upon]

[Hadith 24]

Abu Hurairah ﷺ reported: the Messenger of Allah ﷺ said:

« يَضْحَكُ اللهُ سُبْحَانَهُ وَتَعَالَى إِلَى رَجُلَيْنِ يَقْتُلُ أَحَدُهُمَا الآخَرَ يَدْخُلَانِ الجَنَّةَ ، يُقَاتِلُ هَذَا فِي سَبِيلِ اللهِ فَيُقْتَل ، ثُمَّ يَتُوبُ اللهُ عَلَى الْقَاتِلِ فَيُسْلِمُ فيستشهدُ » مُتَّفَقٌ عَلَيْهِ .

Allah, the Exalted, smiles at two men, one of them killed the other and both will enter Jannah. The first is killed by the other while he is fighting in the Cause of Allah, and thereafter Allah will turn in mercy to the second and guide him to accept Islam and then he dies as a Shaheed (martyr) fighting in the Cause of Allah." [Agreed Upon]

[EXPLANATION OF HADITHS 23 AND 24]

So these two narrations clearly indicate that any individual who makes repentance to Allah, whatsoever that sin or wrongdoing may be, for sure the Exalted and Most High will accept it as He the Exalted says in the Qur'an:

وَٱلَّذِينَ لَا يَدْعُونَ مَعَ ٱللَّهِ إِلَـٰهًا ءَاخَرَ وَلَا يَقْتُلُونَ ٱلنَّفْسَ ٱلَّتِي حَرَّمَ ٱللَّهُ إِلَّا بِٱلْحَقِّ وَلَا يَزْنُونَ ۚ وَمَن يَفْعَلْ ذَٰلِكَ يَلْقَ أَثَامًا ۞ يُضَـٰعَفْ لَهُ ٱلْعَذَابُ يَوْمَ ٱلْقِيَـٰمَةِ وَيَخْلُدْ فِيهِۦ مُهَانًا ۞ إِلَّا مَن تَابَ وَءَامَنَ وَعَمِلَ عَمَلًا صَـٰلِحًا فَأُوْلَـٰئِكَ يُبَدِّلُ ٱللَّهُ سَيِّئَاتِهِمْ حَسَنَـٰتٍ ۗ وَكَانَ ٱللَّهُ غَفُورًا رَّحِيمًا

"And those who invoke not any other ilah (god) along with Allah, nor kill such life as Allah has forbidden, except for a just cause, nor commit illegal sexual intercourse, and whoever does this shall receive the punishment; the torment will be doubled to him on the Day of Resurrection, and he will abide therein in disgrace, except those who repent and believe (in Islamic Monotheism), and do righteous deeds; for those, Allah will change their sins into good deeds, and Allah is Oft-Forgiving, Most Merciful." (Al-Furqaan, 68-70)

Regarding the first narration from Ibn Abbas ⌘, that the son of Adam is never content or satisfied, always desiring more and more wealth; if he has a valley: "He would desire to have two."

Meaning he, being never satisfied, would only wish and desire to have yet another valley. "Nothing can fill his mouth except the earth (of his grave)." And this means, when he dies and is buried, in this case, that is when such great craving and yearning for these things will all stop and come to an end. So for this reason the Prophet ﷺ encouraged repentance. As greatly yearning over that which is required for wealth, will surely make an individual become completely blinded as to how he obtains his wealth or income, so repentance is surely something that the servant is in great need of. So for this reason the Prophet ﷺ said: "Allah turns with mercy to him who turns to Him in repentance."

As for the second narration: Abu Hurairah ﷺ reported that the Messenger of Allah ﷺ said: "Allah, the Exalted, smiles at two men, one of them killed the other and both will enter Jannah. The first is killed by the other while he is fighting in the Cause of Allah, and thereafter Allah will turn in mercy to the second and guide him to accept Islam and then he dies as a Shaheed (martyr) fighting in the Cause of Allah."

So the reason why Allah the Exalted smiles is due to the enmity between these two individuals in the world, to the point that one of them kills the other, so the Exalted removes that which is in both their hearts from animosity, as the people of Paradise carry no such traits in their hearts; Allah says in the Qur'an regarding this and in describing the people of Paradise:

$$\text{وَيَوْمَ نُسَيِّرُ ٱلْجِبَالَ وَتَرَى ٱلْأَرْضَ بَارِزَةً وَحَشَرْنَٰهُمْ فَلَمْ نُغَادِرْ مِنْهُمْ}$$

$$\text{أَحَدًا}$$

"And We shall remove from their breasts any sense of injury (that they may have), (so they will be like) brothers facing each other on thrones." (Al-Hijr, 47)

So this is the reason why Allah smiles.

So this narration is a proof clearly indicating that if a disbeliever embraces Islam, even after having killed a Muslim, Allah the Exalted will accept his repentance, as is known that embracing Islam wipes away one's previous wrongdoings or sins.

باب تحريم الغيبة وباب تحريم النميمة

THE CHAPTERS ON THE PROHIBITION
OF BACKBITING AND TALEBEARING

[THE DEFINITION OF BACKBITING]

So the author (Imam An-Nawawi) starts this chapter which is entitled (in full) "The prohibition of Al-Ghibah (backbiting) and the commandment of guarding one's tongue." Regarding the meaning of the word "backbiting", then the Prophet ﷺ explained this in the following Hadith, when he asked some of his companions: "Do you know what backbiting is?" The companions said: "Allah and His Messenger know better." There upon he said:

«ذِكْرُكَ أَخَاكَ بِمَا يَكْرَهُ»

"Backbiting is talking about your (Muslim) brother in a manner he dislikes."

It was said to him: "What if my (Muslim) brother is as I say?" He ﷺ replied:

«إِنْ كَانَ فِيهِ مَا تَقُولُ فَقَدِ اغْتَبْتَهُ ، وإِنْ لَّمْ يَكُنْ فِيهِ مَا تَقُولُ فَقَدْ بَهَتَّهُ»

"If he is actually as you say, then that is backbiting; but if that is not in him, it is slandering."

So backbiting is regarded as one of the major sins, no prayer, and no charity, fast or any other righteous deed can be done as a means to expiate for it, it stays and remains with that backbiter and is added to his scales (of bad deeds).

Ibn Abdil-Qawi said in a line of poetry:

وَقَدْ قِيلَ غِيبَةٌ نَيمَةٌ   وَكِلْتَاهُمَا كُبْرَى عَلَى نَصِّ أَحْمَدِ

"It is said for sure, backbiting and tale-bearing, both are considered major sins by way of what Ahmed narrates."

This is referring to Ahmed ibn Hanbal ﷺ; i.e. Hadiths recorded by Imam Ahmed, declaring backbiting to be from the major sins. So, the Prophet ﷺ defined backbiting as talking about your brother in a manner he dislikes, and this includes mentioning those things related to a person having some fault in his character or some of that person's short-comings in his religious practises or something general - whatever an individual would detest a person talking about behind his back, then this is considered a form of backbiting.

So pertaining to one of the types of faults in a person, is his character, and that could by way of a person saying similar statements like: "So-and-so is cripple, or lame," or "So-and-so is one eyed, or blind," or the saying: "So-and-so is very tall, or very short," and the likes; this is one type of backbiting. As for the second type, then it is related to a person's character and related to some of his shortcomings in his Deen (religious practices) such as saying: "So-and-so is not chaste" – meaning: he stares at women or beardless handsome boys and the likes. And also included in this is the saying about a person: "So-and-so has many short comings in his Deen," or "So-and-so is a deviant," or the saying, "So-and-so does not pray in the Masjid with the congregation."

So the saying "so-and-so does not do such-and-such matter" and you mention some of his (or her) faults, this is included from the categories of Al-Ghibah. The reason why is because you have mentioned such-and-such matter about him behind his back. But on the other hand, if you say such things about him regarding any of his faults while that individual is present and in front of you, this is not considered Al-Ghibah but it is revilement. Regarding the Prophet's ﷺ statement:

« إنْ كانَ فِيهِ ما تَقُولُ فَقَدِ اغْتَبْتَه ، وإنْ لَمْ يكُنْ فِيهِ ما تَقُولُ فَقَدْ بَهَتَّهُ»

"If he is actually as you say, then that is backbiting; but if that is not in him, that is slandering."

So what this means is, as well as backbiting him, you have also slandered him. And for sure Al-Ghibah may somewhat differ in degree and severity of sin, depending on who it is that is being backbitten! So what we mean by this is, the backbiting of a lay-man is not the same as a scholar, a leader, ruler or minister being backbitten. This is because backbiting the lay-man only affects that individual who is backbitten whereas the backbiting of those in power or the rulers and the likes, if such figures are spoken of wrongly among the masses and they are defamed, for sure this will affect their status among the people as well as influence among the masses.

For example, if a person backbites one of the scholars, this for certain will affect that scholar personally and is counted as a great wrong, but it is counted as a greater wrong due to the fact that this scholar is conveying the Deen to the masses of the Muslims. If this Scholar is backbitten, this makes the people dislike him as well as have an aversion towards him and for sure he will be abandoned by the people who will refrain from referring to him for their legal rulings pertaining to the Deen. This is without doubt a great crime committed and wrong against the Deen.

The backbiting of those in charge of the Muslims, such as the rulers, kings or ministers, is for sure a wrongdoing to them personally, but at the same time, this will certainly corrupt their status as figureheads in charge of the people and the people's hearts will have aversion towards them. And this individual being backbitten, those under his rule will also be greatly affected be him being backbitten, for it will cause them to be divided among themselves, so we say:

وَالْيَوْمُ يُكُونَ رَمِيًّا بالكَلام   وَ غَداً يُكُونَ رَمِيًّا بالسِّهام

"So today speech (will) be hurdled; whilst tomorrow arrows will be shot."

So, if you backbite one of the senior individuals in power who have a high position and authority, this will certainly be a wrongdoing to the Muslims in general, as the body of the Muslims is one, and united, so this will certainly harm them too, whilst they are unaware and perceive it not. The people might think that it is good to backbite the authorities, and vent their dissatisfaction by reviling them, which will change the atmosphere from a state of peace to one of fear and fright.

So we say in short, if your hearts are full of animosity, and you focus on reviling these people, for sure this will first afflict you before them. And maybe the backbiter who reviles people may say: "My intention is to order good and forbid wrong!" We say: for sure this is a good intention you have! However, you must do such matters in the most correct and amicable manner. As the way to do this, is certainly not by exposing and spreading the mistakes and short comings of those in authority faults. So rectify yourself firstly so those around you will be similar.

This seems to be occurring a lot and has affected the Muslims greatly. It has become a simple matter to those affected by reviling those in power as well as the scholars. And such people have not made any improvements to those they have backbitten, and they have not judged them justly as Allah the Exalted commands in the Qur'an:

يَـٰٓأَيُّهَا ٱلَّذِينَ ءَامَنُوا۟ كُونُوا۟ قَوَّٰمِينَ لِلَّهِ شُهَدَآءَ بِٱلْقِسْطِ ۖ وَلَا

يَجْرِمَنَّكُمْ شَنَـَٔانُ قَوْمٍ عَلَىٰٓ أَلَّا تَعْدِلُوا۟

"O you who believe! Stand out firmly for Allah and be just witnesses and let not the enmity and hatred of others make you avoid justice. Be just." (Al-Maa'idah, 8)

So Allah says, let not the enmity and hatred of others make any of you avoid justice. And what is very strange regarding these people (who backbite), is that you never hear them addressing those matters of great concern that are affecting the society either openly, or privately! You never see them rebuking the people who are involved in cheating, lying, etc. when for sure these things are widespread. No, you don't see these backbiting individuals venting their anger out at these wrongdoers in his society. And there is not a shadow of a doubt that the rectification of the youth who indulge in backbiting, if through them refraining from these evil practices; for sure society will slowly start to reform and many great changes will occur in the Ummah.

But with regret there are those who a have very sick type of heart, and seem to love spreading the faults of the scholars and leaders. These troublemakers go around spreading their shortcomings and not ever highlighting any of their good deeds, so we say: glory be to Allah! Is this Just? In the Qur'an Allah says in light of this:

وَٱللَّهُ يَقُولُ ٱلْحَقَّ وَهُوَ يَهْدِى ٱلسَّبِيلَ

"But Allah says the truth, and He guides to the (Right) Way." (Al-Ahzaab, 4)

And even when dealing with the polytheists, the Exalted says:

وَإِذَا فَعَلُواْ فَٰحِشَةً قَالُواْ وَجَدْنَا عَلَيْهَآ ءَابَآءَنَا وَٱللَّهُ أَمَرَنَا بِهَا

"And when they commit a Fahisha (evil deed, going around the Ka'bah in a naked state, every kind of unlawful sexual intercourse, etc.), they say: 'We found our father doing it, and Allah has commanded us of it.'" (Al-A'raaf, 28)

So they said two words, and the first is: **"We found our father doing it"** and the second is: **"And Allah has commanded us of it."** So Allah replies to their empty claims by saying:

إِنَّ ٱللَّهَ لَا يَأْمُرُ بِٱلْفَحْشَآءِ

"Nay, Allah never commands Fahisha."

So here the Exalted accepted the truth from them and what was that? That was that their fathers were those who started the falsehood of idol worshiping. So if it be the case that you desire to speak justice then do so, but as for going out in search for the faults of your brother in faith, especially those in authority, then know for sure, that it is certainly feared that Allah Himself will surely expose your own faults and disgrace you for sure, even it be while you are in your mother's home!

So, that which we have to take great heed of is: avoiding Al-Ghibah and restraining our tongues; we must not forget that every time a person backbites another person, this decrease the backbiter's good deeds! And at the same time, it increases the person who is being backbitten in good deeds and this is confirmed by the Prophet's ﷺ statement in the following Hadith:

«أَتَدْرُونَ مِنَ الْمُفْلِسُ ؟» قَالُوا : الْمُفْلِسُ فِينَا مَنْ لا دِرْهَمَ لَهُ وَلا مَتَاعَ. فقال : « إِنَّ الْمُفْلِسَ مِنْ أُمَّتِي مَنْ يَأْتِي يَوْمَ الْقِيَامَةِ بِصَلاةٍ وَصِيَامٍ وَزَكَاةٍ، وَيَأْتِي وَقَدْ شَتَمَ هَذَا، وقذَف هَذَا وَأَكَلَ مالَ هَذَا، وسَفَكَ دَم هَذَا ، وَضَرَبَ هَذَا، فَيُعْطَى هَذَا مِنْ حسَنَاتِهِ، وَهَذَا مِنْ حسَنَاتِهِ، فَإِنْ فَنِيَتْ حسناته قَبْلَ أَنْ يَقْضِيَ مَا عَلَيْهِ، أُخِذَ مِنْ خَطَايَاهُمْ فَطُرِحَتْ عليْهِ، ثُمَّ طُرِح فِي النَّارِ»

"Do you know who the bankrupt one is?" The [companions] said: "The bankrupt one among us is one who has neither money with him nor any property." He (ﷺ) said: "The real bankrupt one of my Ummah is the one who would come on the Day of Resurrection with Salaat (prayer), Saum (fasting), and Sadaqah (charity), because he reviled others, brought calumny against others, unlawfully devoured the wealth of others, shed the blood of others and beat others; so his good deeds would be credited to the accounts of those (who suffered at his hand). If his good deeds fall short to clear the account, their sins would be entered in his account and he would be thrown in the (Hell) fire."

And it is narrated from some of the Salaf, that when it reached them that someone had backbitten them, they would send a gift to that individual who had backbitten them, so when that gift had reached the backbiter, he would say: "Who has sent me this?" So it would reach him that "the person you had backbitten, heard you had backbitten him, so he said: 'I heard that you had given me your good deeds as a gift, which I will certainly benefit from on the Day of Judgment, so I give you this gift so that in this world you benefit from them, but the next life is the abode of reward and punishment.'"

So brother, my advice to you is to distance yourself as far as you can from Al-Ghibah as well as discussing matters related to the rulers, scholars and other than them; but if you must be a peacemaker, trying to mend the Muslims' affairs, and if you are unable to achieve that, then tend to yourselves, and that is by rectifying your own affairs.

We ask, does backbiting any of the scholars or those in authority bring about any change or even rectify any of the situations the Muslims are encountering? Never! Rather it creates more problems. So if this is the case, then refrain from circulating bad propaganda, rather, spread good things among the people. And that is just, as justice is defined as neither being too much inclined to this way nor inclining too much towards that way. May Allah grant us and you good and that which leads to good and rectification!

Allah ﷻ says in the Qur'an:

وَلَا يَغْتَب بَّعْضُكُم بَعْضًا ۚ أَنُحِبُّ أَحَدُكُمْ أَن يَأْكُلَ لَحْمَ أَخِيهِ مَيْتًا

فَكَرِهْتُمُوهُ ۚ وَٱتَّقُوا ٱللَّهَ ۚ إِنَّ ٱللَّهَ تَوَّابٌ رَّحِيمٌ

"And backbite not one another. Would one of you like to eat the flesh of his dead brother? You would hate it (so hate backbiting). And fear Allah. Verily, Allah is the One who forgives and accepts repentance, the Most Merciful." (Al-Hujuraat, 12)

Also Allah the Exalted says:

وَلَا تَقْفُ مَا لَيْسَ لَكَ بِهِۦ عِلْمٌ ۚ إِنَّ ٱلسَّمْعَ وَٱلْبَصَرَ وَٱلْفُؤَادَ كُلُّ أُوْلَٰٓئِكَ

كَانَ عَنْهُ مَسْئُولاً

"And follow not (O man, i.e., say not or do not or witness not) that of which you have no knowledge. Verily, the hearing, and the sight, and the heart of each of those ones will be questioned (by Allah)." (Al-Isra', 36)

Also the Exalted says:

مَّا يَلْفِظُ مِن قَوْلٍ إِلَّا لَدَيْهِ رَقِيبٌ عَتِيدٌ

"Not a word does he (or she) utter, but there is a watcher by him ready (to record)." (Qaaf, 18)

[EXPLANATION OF SUPPORTING VERSES]

So the author (Imam An-Nawawi) mentions verses relating to the subject at hand, and the first of these is the words of Allah ﷻ when He says:

وَلَا يَغْتَب بَّعْضُكُم بَعْضًا

"And backbite not one another…"

The full verse reads:

يَٰٓأَيُّهَا ٱلَّذِينَ ءَامَنُوا۟ ٱجْتَنِبُوا۟ كَثِيرًا مِّنَ ٱلظَّنِّ إِنَّ بَعْضَ ٱلظَّنِّ إِثْمٌ

وَلَا تَجَسَّسُوا۟ وَلَا يَغْتَب بَّعْضُكُم بَعْضًا أَيُحِبُّ أَحَدُكُمْ أَن يَأْكُلَ

لَحْمَ أَخِيهِ مَيْتًا فَكَرِهْتُمُوهُ

"O you who believe! Avoid much suspicion; indeed some suspicions are sins. And spy not, neither backbite not one another. Would one of you like to eat the flesh of his dead brother? You would hate it (so hate backbiting)." (Al-Hujuraat, 12)

Allah the Exalted forbids Al-Ghibah, then He gives an example so as to make people have an aversion toward it and shun this detested act: **"Would one of you like to eat the flesh of his dead brother? You would hate it."** So, if your dead Muslim brother was presented to you to eat, would you eat him? The answer is certainly not! And without doubt, everyone would answer this the same way. And if it was said, what significance does this example have pertaining to

72

backbiting? We say, the significance it has is that the individual that you backbite, due to him being absent, is unable to defend himself, just like a person's body part if it was to be cut off, it would also be unable to defend itself. If you spoke badly about your brother while he is present, this would not be considered backbiting, rather it would be referred to as you cursing, swearing or abusing him. And the same verse ends with:

وَٱتَّقُوا۟ ٱللَّهَ إِنَّ ٱللَّهَ تَوَّابٌ رَّحِيمٌ

"And fear Allah. Verily, Allah is the One Who forgives and accepts repentance, Most Merciful."

So here Allah the Exalted commands us to fear Him after forbidding the act of backbiting, and this indicates, that those who backbite others have not feared Allah ﷻ; so know, O dear Muslim! If you are in the habit of spreading your brother's faults among the people, then Allah will certainly expose your own faults and make them known among the people, as the Prophet ﷺ said in a Hadith:

مَنْ تتبع عَورَة أَخِيهِ تتبع الله عَورَتِهِ, وَمَنْ تتبع الله عَورَتِهِ فضحه وَلَوْ فِي بَيْتِ أُمِهِ

"Whosoever pursues the faults of his brother, Allah will pursue his faults and whosoever pursues his brothers faults Allah will expose his faults even if he be in the depths of his home."

But, in saying this, if exposing an individual is done as a means of advice and clarification, then in this case it would be permissible. And we will give you an example of what we mean: say a person come to you for advice and enquiring about doing business with a certain individual, so he says to you: "What do you think of so-and-so? Should I go into business with him or not?" If you knew that individual who is being inquired about, and that he falls very short and is not worthy of going in to business with, in this case it would be perfectly allowed for you to clarify to the questioner that this person is bad to do business with, as this will come under advising him from falling prey to this person's wrongdoings; the proof for this is the Hadith where there companions proposed to Fatimah bint Qais, namely: Usamah Ibn Zaid, Mu'awiyah ibn Abi Sufyaan and Abu Jahm; so she went to the Prophet ﷺ seeking his advice saying "so-and-so and so-and-so have proposed to me," so the Prophet ﷺ said to her:

أَمَّا مُعَاوِيَةُ ، فَصُعْلُوكٌ لا مالَ له ، وأَمَّا أَبو الجَهْم فلا يضَعُ العَصا عنْ عاتِقِهِ أَنْكِحِهي أُسَامَة

"As for Mu'awiyah he is poor and he has no property, and as for Abu Jahm, his stick never leaves his side (he beats women). Marry Usamah."

So here the Prophet ﷺ mentioned two disliked qualities in these two men, but not as to spread or expose their shortcomings or faults, but rather as a form of advice. So there is a difference pertaining to this type of matter. We'll give you another type of example: if someone came to you, seeking advice regarding seeking knowledge from a certain individual, and you knew this individual has problems in his creed and methodology, then in this case it would be allowed for you to point them out to that individual, based upon what you know about his problems. So you would be perfectly allowed to say, "This individual has errors in his Aqeedah (beliefs)," or "this individual's views are incorrect," or point out his deviations in his methodology; you would be permitted to expose this individual based upon the face that these errors might rub off on the questioner seeking your advice.

When such types of clarifications are not made, there is a high possibility that this individual's errors, deviations and misguidance will spread among the people, and there are many examples we could mention regarding this. So in short, if you are advising an individual regarding someone's fault from the angle of clarification and advice, then it is allowed for you.

There is a statement spread among the masses of people that states: "The sinful one is okay to backbite." This statement is neither a Hadith nor an accepted statement! Rather, the sinful individual is like anyone else, he has rights too, and he is forbidden to be backbitten! But if need be, he can be exposed for the benefit of the general public, for it would be allowed to warn about this sinful individual's conduct, and we say this could even be obligatory at times. This statement regarding the backbiting of the sinful wrongdoer is incorrect and not something the Prophet ﷺ had stated.

Regarding the second verse from the three that the author (Imam An-Nawawi) mentions, then it is the statement of Allah ﷺ when He says:

$$ وَلَا تَقْفُ مَا لَيْسَ لَكَ بِهِۦ عِلْمٌ ۚ إِنَّ ٱلسَّمْعَ وَٱلْبَصَرَ وَٱلْفُؤَادَ كُلُّ أُوْلَٰٓئِكَ كَانَ عَنْهُ مَسْـُٔولًا $$

"And follow not (O man, i.e., say not or do not or witness not) that of which you have no knowledge. Verily, the hearing, and the sight, and the heart of

each of those ones will be questioned (by Allah)."
(Al-Isra', 36)

"And follow not" means: do not involve yourself in matters you have no knowledge regarding. And this refers to all matters, so stay away from them. It also pertains to discussing and involving oneself in explaining knowledge-matters related to Allah and His Messenger ﷺ. And although this prohibition is general, the most severe type is talking about Allah and His Messenger ﷺ without knowledge.

An example for this is that you say, "Allah the Exalted said such-and-such," when in actual fact, it is the opposite and Allah never said such a thing, or you attempt to comment or explain something based upon your desires from the meaning of the Qur'an; in such a case, you would have said about Allah that which you have no knowledge of. Therefore, it is impermissible for a Muslim to try to explain the Book of Allah without knowledge, as this is equal to saying that Allah Himself intends such-and-such meaning from such-and-such verse, or this is how Allah wants us to understand such-and-such verse.

Such false claims regarding the Qur'an are counted as tremendous grave errors so it is upon the Muslim to avoid commenting about the Deen without sure knowledge, as well as other matters he has little knowledge regarding. And Allah ﷻ has linked *Shirk* and talking about Allah without knowledge in terms of severity when He says in the following verse in the Qur'an:

قُل إِنَّمَا حَرَّمَ رَبِّيَ ٱلْفَوَاحِشَ مَا ظَهَرَ مِنْهَا وَمَا بَطَنَ وَٱلْإِثْمَ وَٱلْبَغْىَ

بِغَيْرِ ٱلْحَقِّ وَأَن تُشْرِكُوا بِٱللَّهِ مَا لَمْ يُنَزِّلْ بِهِۦ سُلْطَٰنًا وَأَن تَقُولُوا عَلَى

ٱللَّهِ مَا لَا تَعْلَمُونَ

"Say (O Muhammad): '(But) the things that my Lord has indeed forbidden are *Al-Fawaahish* (great evil sins, every kind of unlawful sexual intercourse etc.), whether committed openly or secretly, sins (of all kinds), oppression, joining partners (in worship) with Allah for which He has given no authority, and to say about Allah of which you have no knowledge." (Al-A'raaf, 33)

And the same is said if you talk about others without knowledge, that is you say, "So-and-so said such-and-such," when that individual in actual fact never said such a statement. Do not rely upon information until it is first verified, especially when information is regarding a certain matter being propagated among the people; in this case, it becomes binding on a person to safeguard himself even more.

And that which has befallen the masses is idle gossip. For some strange reason the people make a mountain out of nothing and exaggerate and turn one word into any many and they seem to make something out of nothing. And few seem to be able to protect themselves from falling prey to this. And for sure, much of what is circulated from the speech of many people is nothing more than false tales, from nothing but their sheer whims and desires, and we seek Allah's refuge from this, about matters they know little or nothing about!

Regarding the third and last verse, it is the statement of Allah the Exalted:

وَلَقَدْ خَلَقْنَا ٱلْإِنسَـٰنَ وَنَعْلَمُ مَا تُوَسْوِسُ بِهِۦ نَفْسُهُۥ ۖ وَنَحْنُ أَقْرَبُ إِلَيْهِ مِنْ حَبْلِ ٱلْوَرِيدِ • إِذْ يَتَلَقَّى ٱلْمُتَلَقِّيَانِ عَنِ ٱلْيَمِينِ وَعَنِ ٱلشِّمَالِ قَعِيدٌ • مَّا يَلْفِظُ مِن قَوْلٍ إِلَّا لَدَيْهِ رَقِيبٌ عَتِيدٌ

"And indeed We created man, and We know what his own self whispers to him; and We are nearer to him than his jugular vein (by Our knowledge); (remember!) that the two receivers (recording angels) receive (each human after he or she has attained the age of puberty), one sitting on his right and one sitting on his left (to note his or her actions); not a word does he (or she) utter, but there is a watcher by him ready (to record it)." (Qaaf, 16-18)

The author mentions only this portion but it would have been better for him to mention the verses leading up to it as Allah ﷻ mentions He created mankind and He knows all His Creation, just as He says in the Qur'an:

أَلَا يَعْلَمُ مَنْ خَلَقَ وَهُوَ ٱللَّطِيفُ ٱلْخَبِيرُ

"Should not He Who has created know, and He is Most Kind and Courteous." (Al-Mulk, 14)

The Exalted knows every individual's condition, intentions, resting places and every matter relating to mankind; as for Allah's words: **"And We know what his own self whispers to him,"** it means: Allah the Exalted knows whatever an individual utters to himself, or his secret thoughts, and He knows these thoughts before a person even thinks them; but in saying this an individual is not taken to account for what his own self whispers to him, but if that thought crossed his mind, and he dwelled on it, believing it to be reality and something he should now follow, in this case, he is held to account for it. But as we said, one will not be taken to account for those thoughts or whispers that overcome him, as the Prophet ﷺ said:

إِنَّ اللهَ تَجَاوَزَ عَنْ أُمَّتِي مَا حَدَّثَتْ بِهِ أَنْفسهَا مَا لَمْ تَعْمل أَوْ تَتَكَلم

"Indeed Allah has forgiven my nation the thoughts (one has) so long as he does not act upon them or utter them."

We will give an example pertaining to one getting whispers or doubtful thoughts: say an individual got whispers that he should divorce his wife; many think that the mere thought of such a thing automatically makes the wife divorced, but such thoughts do not divorce one's wife unless the individual has verbally stated so or written that in a statement indicating his intent as well as his statement. Allah ﷻ has forgiven one's thoughts so long as one does not act upon them or talk about them, as He ﷻ says:

وَلَقَدْ خَلَقْنَا ٱلْإِنسَٰنَ وَنَعْلَمُ مَا تُوَسْوِسُ بِهِۦ نَفْسُهُۥ ۖ وَنَحْنُ أَقْرَبُ إِلَيْهِ مِنْ حَبْلِ ٱلْوَرِيدِ • إِذْ يَتَلَقَّى ٱلْمُتَلَقِّيَانِ عَنِ ٱلْيَمِينِ وَعَنِ ٱلشِّمَالِ قَعِيدٌ

"And indeed We created man, and We know what his own self whispers to him, And We are nearer to him than his jugular vein (by Our knowledge);

(remember!) that the two receivers (recording angels) receive (each human after he or she has attained the age of puberty), one sitting on his right and one sitting on his left (to note his or her actions)." (Qaaf 16-17)

So Allah the Exalted and High has appointed two angels to every person, one on his right and the other on his left, always present with them recording every word or statement he utters and every deed he commits; Allah says:

$$\text{مَّا يَلْفِظُ مِن قَوْلٍ إِلَّا لَدَيْهِ رَقِيبٌ عَتِيدٌ}$$

"Not a word does he (or she) utter, but there is a watcher by him ready (to record it)." (Qaaf, 18)

What this means is, no matter what an individual says, this is surely recorded by those watchers over him. Regarding the word: "watcher," it means: "supervisor or watcher." As for the next word: "ready (to record it)," it means this watcher is always present with a person, never leaving him; we say this is like you owning a recorder that records, which you place into your pocket to record all that you will say. For sure if this was the case, when you listen back to your own speech, you would be completely astonished with the things you were talking about without a care in the world! And a person may utter a word giving it no thought and by that, one obtains Allah's displeasure and is thrown due to that statement into the Hell Fire the distance of such-and-such, and we seek Allah refuge!

We will mention to you what is narrated about Imam Ahmed ibn Hanbal ﷺ during his sickness, and one of his companions came to visit him at his home while he was in a lot of pain and groaning due to the severe pain from that sickness; his companion said to him, "so-and-so individual from the successors of the companions of the Prophet ﷺ said, 'Certainly, the angels record everything, even a sick individual's groaning during his sickness.'" Imam Ahmed refrained immediately from groaning out of fear that the angel may record that against him. So this shows that it is binding upon every individual to minimise his speech as much as he is able as the Prophet ﷺ said:

مَنْ كَانَ يُؤْمِنُ بِاللَّهِ وَالْيَوْمِ الآخِرِ فَلْيَقُلْ خَيْرًا أَوْ لِيَصْمُتْ

"He who believes in Allah and the Last Day must either speak good or remain silent."

So the meaning of the words "either speak good" is that one should speak only good in a gathering, and what this means is either within the words a person speaks is good or they lead to and create harmony, affection and brings about a closer bond; and the opposite is that is if you came upon a gathering of people and remained sitting in complete silence, there is a high possibility that they may prefer to avoid sitting with you due to this (so there should be a balance between the two).

"Either speak good or remain silent." This refers to refraining from that which could be recorded against a person from the many things he could utter; so regarding Al-Ghibah, be cautious, wary, vigilant and on your guard from falling into it, and know that it is something being written against you. If you backbite an individual in this life, on the Day Judgement, he will take your good deeds from you until you have no deeds left and if that becomes the case, his bad deeds will be transferred to you and this could be a cause for you to be thrown into the Hell-Fire.

So understand, after hearing what we have said, that it is binding upon the Muslim to safeguard his tongue from all forms of speech except that which is of benefit; but on the other hand if what you will say is mixed, meaning it has some good as well as some bad, then the guidance of the Prophet ﷺ is to refrain from that speech, because there is a possibility that what is said could lead to something which is forbidden. And this seems to be the case in these times with most people's words. So we say remaining silent is better and it is also safer and there is nothing is equal to that. Allah grants success!

[Hadith 1511]

Abu Hurairah ❀ reported that the Prophet ﷺ said:

« مَنْ كَانَ يُؤْمِنُ بِاللَّهِ وَاليَوْمِ الآخِرِ فَلْيَقُلْ خَيْراً ، أُوْ لِيَصْمُتْ » متفقٌ عليه.

"He who believes in Allah and the Last Day must either speak good or remain silent." [Agreed Upon]

[Hadith 1512]

Abu Musa Al-Ash'ari ❀ reported: I asked the Messenger of Allah ﷺ who is the most excellent among the Muslims? He (ﷺ) said:

« مَنْ سَلِمَ المُسْلِمُونَ مِن لِسَانِهِ وَيَدِهِ » . متفق عليه .

"One from whose tongue and hands the other Muslims are secure." [Agreed Upon]

[EXPLANATION OF 1511 AND 1512]

The author (Imam An-Nawawi) mentions these two narrations pertaining to backbiting, so know, it is a must upon every Muslim to safeguard and preserve his (her) tongue from all forms of speech, with the exception of virtuous beneficial speech that brings about a benefit in this life or the next, as this is what we understand from the Prophet's ﷺ statement: "He who believes in Allah and the Last Day must either speak good or remain silent."

Regarding this Hadith, we say: if you decide to talk about any matter, and you are unsure as to whether what you are going to say is a good thing or not, it would be advisable to completely withhold from saying anything altogether! This is because it is safer, and nothing is equal to silence! On the other hand, if a matter entails that you have to speak, then do so. And this could be related to something which you may have witnessed, like some wrong taking place. In this case, silence is not preferred. Rather it would become an obligation upon you to speak out against this wrong. So know that the statement of the Prophet ﷺ indicates that it is an obligation upon a person to remain silent if he has nothing good to say!

The Prophet ﷺ made it a condition that the faith in a person depends upon what he utters, as well as refrains from. And "good" is of two types:

The first type is verbal utterances of worship such as glorifying, exalting and magnifying Allah the Exalted, as well as the reciting of the Qur'an, teaching the Deen, etc.

The second type is verbally inciting towards good. This is includes general beneficial words such as inciting harmony as well as unity among the people, as well as making one's Muslim brothers (or sisters) happy and joyful in a gathering. All of this is counted as something considered a good noble act.

As we alluded to earlier, if an individual remained completely silent until the gathering ends, whatever gathering it may be for, the people will surely consider him as boring, unsociable and they may even come to dislike him. But if he were to say lawful things which incite them toward good as well as words that will make them feel delighted, then this is also adding to what we have already said. On the other hand, if he were to utter statements which make the people laugh whilst lying, there is a fear that such an individual falls under a severe threat as mentioned in a narration where the Prophet ﷺ said:

وَيْلٌ لِلَّذِي يُحَدِّثُ فَيَكْذِبُ لِيُضْحِكَ بِهِ القَوْمَ, وَيْلٌ لَهُ, ثُمَّ وَيْلٌ لَهُ

"Woe to him who lies in his talk to make the people laugh. Woe to him! Woe to him!"

So this is what some individuals do which they call: "Cracking jokes". This is how some people amuse themselves and they do this in the name of making the people happy and delighted. But in saying this, if this is done in a lawful manner to increase the people happiness, then there is no problem in doing so, but if this is done by way of an individual lying then this is totally impermissible.

The author next mentions the narration wherein Abu Musa Al-Ash'ari reported that he asked the Messenger of Allah ﷺ who the most excellent among the Muslims is? The Prophet ﷺ replied: "One from whose tongue and hands the other

Muslims are secure." What this means is, do not wrong other Muslims, such as by backbiting, talebearing, reviling, cursing and anything of this nature. And as for the words: "and hands," this means one avoids taking or stealing people's wealth, or hitting and beating them. Rather, he is a just individual, and he (or she) deals with people on amicable terms and he does unto people similar to how he wishes them to deal with him. This for sure is the Muslim. So this Hadith is a strong incitement for one to preserve and safeguard his tongue and to withhold his hands from harming the people.

Safeguarding the tongue is refraining it from talking about other Muslims, and only uttering good about them, and is, as we said, to refrain one's hands from harming them physically and avoiding taking peoples wealth unjustly. Rather be peaceful and free from oppressing others, this is the ideal Muslim as well as the best Muslim.

[Hadith 1513]

Sahl ibn Sa'd ﷺ reported that the Messenger of Allah ﷺ said:

« مَنْ يَضْمَنْ لِي مَا بَيْنَ لَحْيَيْهِ وَمَا بَيْنَ رِجْلَيْهِ أَضْمَنْ لَهُ الجَنَّة » . متفقٌ عليهِ .

"Whosoever gives me a guarantee to safeguard what is between his jaws and what is between his legs, I shall guarantee him Paradise." [Agreed Upon]

[Hadith 1514]

Abu Hurairah reported: I heard the Prophet ﷺ saying:

«إِنَّ الْعَبْدَ لَيَتَكَلَّمُ بِالكَلِمةِ مَا يَتَبَيَّنُ فِيهَا يَزِلُّ بِهَا إِلى النَّارِ أَبْعَدَ مِمَّا بَيْنَ المشْرِقِ والمغْرِب». متفقٌ عليهِ.

"A person utters a word thoughtlessly and as a result of this, he will fall down into the Fire of Hell deeper than the distance between the east and the west." [Agreed Upon]

[Hadith 1515]

Abu Hurairah reported the Prophet ﷺ said:

« إِنَّ الْعَبْدَ لَيَتَكَلَّمُ بِالكَلِمةِ مِنْ رِضْوَانِ اللهِ تَعَالى مَا يُلْقِي لَهَا بَالاً يَرْفَعُهُ اللهُ بِهَا دَرَجَاتٍ ، وَإِنَّ الْعَبْدَ لَيَتَكَلَّمُ بِالكَلِمةِ مِنْ سَخَطِ اللهِ تَعَالى لا يُلْقِي لَهَا بَالاً يهوِي بِهَا فِي جَهَنَّم » رواه البخاري.

"A man utters a word pleasing to Allah without considering it of any significance for which Allah exalts his ranks (in Jannah); another speaks a word displeasing to Allah without considering it of any importance, and for this reason he will sink down into Hell." [Al-Bukhari]

[EXPLANATION OF HADITHS 1513 TO 1515]

These Hadiths indicate the severity and dangers of the tongue, and that it is the most severe and dangerous of one's organs. The first narration is the statement of the Prophet ﷺ: "Whosoever gives me a guarantee to safeguard what is between his jaws and what is between his legs, I shall guarantee him Paradise." So that which is between one's jaws is the tongue and that which is between one's legs are the private parts, and this Hadith refers two both males and females.

The first thing is the tongue, and that is protecting it from falling into saying that which is Haraam (impermissible), and from these things is lying, backbiting, talebearing, slandering others, cheating, etc. As for the privates, then it is protecting it from falling into fornication, homosexuality, lesbianism and anything which leads to these detestable acts. So the Prophet ﷺ guaranteed the individual Paradise, and this means, it will be that individual's recompense and reward for preserving these two things.

So safeguard your tongue and private parts! The Prophet ﷺ made a connection between the tongue and the private parts, and that is because the tongue can talk about lustful things (which can make a person desire to commit Zina) and some people also get great satisfaction out of talking wrongly about people's honour, and we seek Allah's refuge from this!

As for the second narration then it is the statement of the Prophet ﷺ when he said: "A person utters a word thoughtlessly and, as a result of this, he will fall down into the Fire of Hell deeper than the distance between the east and the west." The meaning "thoughtlessly" means an individual is not certain about the information that his reached him regarding a particular matter which he himself then narrates to others. For this reason the Prophet ﷺ said in another narration:

كَفَى بِالْمَرْءِ كَذِباً أَنْ يُحَدِّثَ بِكُلِّ ما سَمِعَ

"It is enough for a man to prove himself a liar when he goes around narrating whatever he hears."

So you find an individual speaking without giving what he said any thought whatsoever, and he does not ascertaining what is narrated to them nor consider that information has reached him. We seek refuge in Allah for all that leads a person into the Hell-Fire as deep as the east and the west. And the distance between the east and west is for sure very far, and one single word can make a person that deep into the Hell-Fire.

So this is a proof that it is an obligation upon the Muslim to be sure and certain about what he utters regarding any matter. Before you utter any words, or relay information regarding someone or something, first be certain of that thing, be patient instead of hasty and speak not unless you see that there is some benefit in opening your mouth.

Think first to yourself: is there any benefit in me talking about this thing? Whatsoever it may be! And if you come to the conclusion that there is no benefit in speaking about that matter then remain silent as this what the Prophet ﷺ meant when he said: "He who believes in Allah and the Last Day must either speak good or remain silent."

As for the third narration, then what is meant by the Prophet's ﷺ words, "a man utters a word pleasing to Allah" is any act of worship that one may utter, such as glorifying, exalting, and magnifying Allah, as well as reading the Qur'an, ordering good and forbidding evil, teaching people the Deen, making peace between two individuals (or two groups) and the like.

"...Without considering it of any significance for which Allah exalts his ranks (in Jannah)." This means a person may utter a word giving it neither any importance nor significance whatsoever or realising its loftiness. And we say, it could be the case that this individual realises the virtue of what he is saying perhaps due to studying the matter prior, yet he does not think it will elevate him to the level such an utterance can reach with Allah, so due to this Allah admits him into Paradise.

As for the statement of the Prophet ﷺ: "Another speaks a word displeasing to Allah without considering it of any importance, and for this reason he will sink down into Hell," then this means that an individual may say something not giving it any significance or value, without thought of its magnitude in Allah's sight, and due to this he will sink into the Hell-Fire. This is because this person never thought his uttering this statement would reach to the level it reached, and this happens with many people, and we seek refuge with Allah from falling into it! You find a person being asked about an individual that is a bit weak in his Deen and sinful, so when he is asked, he says: "Leave this individual." Or he may say: "By Allah, this individual has no clue about the Deen (the Religion)!" Or he says: "Allah will never forgive so-and-so!" Such statements are very dangerous indeed and it is narrated that a pious worshipper (in the past) passed by an individual who was falling short with regards to his religious obligations, so this pious worshipper said about this sinner: "By Allah,

Allah will not forgive this sinner!" This worshipper restricted something vast by such a statement, and it was the case that this pious worshipper was overly amazed at his own devotion to Allah and his acts of worship, so he considered himself above this sinful individual in the sight of Allah ﷻ. Allah said:

مَنْ ذَا الَّذِي يَأْلِي عَلَيَّ أَنْ لَا أَغْفِرَ لِفُلَانٍ قَدْ غَفَرْتُ لِفُلَانٍ وَأَحْبَطْتُ عَمَلَكَ

"Who is it that says I will not forgive so-and-so? I have forgiven him and invalidated (all) your deeds!"

Allah is the owner of the creation and dominion and He executes any order or command as He pleases. None shares in this except by His leave or command. By one statement the worshipper uttered, all his deeds were nullified completely. We ask Allah for safety! So be very careful about what you utter, be careful regarding the matter pertaining to the tongue!

We will give another example: say so-and-so said to his brother in faith: "I am going to advise my neighbour about abandoning prayer as he does not pray." To which the brother in faith says, "I do not think that he can ever be guided, impossible!" Or "He is a wrongdoer, sinful!" And we seek refuge from such words. We say regarding this: in whose Hands are the hearts of the servants of Allah? Allah ﷻ without doubt, just as the Prophet ﷺ said in a Hadith:

مَا مِنْ قَلْبٍ مِنْ قُلُوبِ بَنِي آدَم إِلَّا بَيْنَ إِصْبَعَيْنِ مِنْ الرَّحْمَن عَزَّ وَجَلَّ يُقَلِّبُهُ كَيْفَ يشاء, إِنْ شَاءَ أَزَاغَهُ وَ إِنْ شَاءَ هَدَاهُ

"There is no heart from the hearts of the sons of Adam except they are between the Fingers of the Most-Merciful. He turns them as He pleases, so if He pleases He can let them go astray and if He pleases he can guide them."

This is something we accept: that the hearts are between the Fingers of the Most-Merciful and He does as He pleases with them. So can one possibly utter the statement, "So-and-so can never be guided"? This is totally forbidden, rather, one should supplicate for that individual to be guided and not give up hope.

Is it not so that there were staunch enemies of Islam who hated it? Is it not so? Is it not true that Umar ibn Khattaab ﷺ was one of them? But he later became the second leader of the Muslims after the Prophet ﷺ! He used to dislike Islam and warn people away from it and hated its followers. Is this not so? Likewise, Khaalid ibn Waleed and Ikramah ibn Abi Jahl, before they embraced Islam! But later on in their lives, they became powerful outstanding leaders which strengthened Islam greatly and its followers. So have faith dear brothers and despair not, and ask Allah ﷺ for firmness and guidance. Keep your tongue away from that which will bring about your destruction. We ask Allah to protect us from falling into disobedience, to grant us success and to that which leads us to His pleasure; indeed He has the ability to do all things!

[Hadith 1516]

Abu AbdurRahmaan Bilaal bin Al-Haarith Al-Muzani reported that the Messenger of Allah ﷺ said:

« إِنَّ الرَّجُلَ لَيَتَكَلَّمُ بِالْكَلِمَةِ مِنْ رِضْوَانِ اللهِ تَعَالَى مَا كَانَ يَظُنُّ أَنْ تَبْلُغَ مَا بَلَغَتْ يَكْتُبُ اللهُ لَهُ بِهَا رِضْوَانَهُ إِلَى يَوْمِ يَلْقَاهُ، وَإِنَّ الرَّجُلَ لَيَتَكَلَّمُ بِالْكَلِمَةِ مِنْ سَخَطِ اللهِ مَا كَانَ يَظُنُّ أَنْ تَبْلُغَ مَا بَلَغَتْ يَكْتُبُ اللهُ لَهُ بِهَا سَخَطَهُ إِلَى يَوْمِ يَلْقَاهُ ». رَوَاهُ مَالِكٌ فِي الْمُوَطَّأِ وَالتِّرْمِذِي وَقَالَ: حَدِيثٌ حَسَنٌ صَحِيحٌ .

"A man speaks a good word without knowing its worth, and Allah records for him His pleasure until the Day he will meet Him; and a man utters an evil word without realising its importance, and Allah records for him His displeasure until the Day he will meet Him." [At-Tirmidhi]

[Hadith 1517]

Sufyaan ibn Abdullah ﷺ reported:

قُلْتُ يَا رَسُولَ اللهِ حَدِّثْنِي بِأَمْرٍ أَعْتَصِمُ بِهِ قَالَ : « قُلْ رَبِّيَ اللهُ ، ثُمَّ اسْتَقِمْ » قُلْتُ : يَا رَسُولَ اللهِ مَا أَخْوَفُ مَا تَخَافُ عَلَيَّ ؟ فَأَخَذَ بِلِسَانِ نَفْسِهِ ، ثُمَّ قَالَ: « هَذَا ». رَوَاهُ التِّرْمِذِي وَقَالَ: حَدِيثٌ حَسَنٌ صَحِيحٌ .

"I said: 'O Messenger of Allah! Tell me, of something to which I may remain steadfast?' He said: 'Say: My Lord is Allah and then remain steadfast.' Then I said: 'O Messenger of Allah! What do you fear most about me?' He took hold of his tongue." [At-Tirmidhi]

[Hadith 1518]

Ibn Umar reported the Messenger of Allah ﷺ said:

« لَا تُكْثِرُوا الْكَلَامَ بِغَيْرِ ذِكْرِ اللهِ، فَإِنَّ كَثْرَةَ الْكَلَامِ بِغَيْرِ ذِكْرِ اللهِ تَعَالَى قَسْوَةٌ لِلْقَلْبِ، وإِنَّ أَبْعَدَ النَّاسِ مِنَ اللهِ الْقَلْبُ الْقَاسِي ». رَوَاهُ التِّرْمِذِي.

"Do indulge in excessive talk except when remembering Allah. Excessive talking without the remembrance of Allah hardens the heart; and those who are the farthest from Allah are those whose hearts are hard." [At-Tirmidhi; Al-Albani graded it weak]

[Hadith 1519]

Abu Hurairah ﷺ reported: the Messenger of Allah ﷺ said:

« مَنْ وَقَاهُ اللهُ شَرَّ مَا بَيْنَ لَحْيَيْهِ ، وشَرَّ مَا بَيْنَ رِجْلَيْهِ دَخَلَ الجَنَّةَ » رَوَاه التِّرمِذي وقال : حديث حسنٌ.

"He whom Allah saves from the evil of that which is between his jaws and the evil of that which is between his legs will enter Paradise." [At-Tirmidhi]

[Hadith 1520]

Uqbah ibn Aamir ﷺ said: I asked the Messenger of Allah ﷺ: "How can salvation be achieved?" He replied:

« أَمْسِكْ عَلَيْكَ لِسانَكَ ، وَلْيَسَعْكَ بيْتُكَ ، وابْكِ على خَطِيئَتِكَ » رواه الترمذي وقالَ: حديثٌ حسنٌ

"Control your tongue, keep to your home, and weep over your sins."

[Hadith 1521]

Abu Sa'id al-Khudri ﷺ said: the Prophet ﷺ said:

« إذا أَصْبَحَ ابْنُ آدم ، فَإِنَّ الأَعْضَاءَ كُلَّهَا تُكَفِّرُ اللِّسَانَ ، تَقُولُ : اتَّقِ اللهَ فِينَا ، فَإِنَّمَا نَحْنُ بِكَ : فَإِنِ اسْتَقَمْتَ اسْتَقَمْنَا وإِنِ اعْوَجَجْتَ اعْوَجَجْنَا » رواه الترمذي .

"When the son of Adam gets up in the morning, all the limbs humble themselves before the tongue and say: 'Fear Allah for our sake because we are with you: (i.e., we will be rewarded or punished as a result of what you do); if you are straight, we will be straight; and if you are crooked, we will become crooked.'" [At-Tirmidhi]

[Hadith 1522]

Mu'adh ibn Jabal ﷺ reported:

قُلْتُ: يا رسُولَ اللَّهِ، أخبِرني بِعَمَلٍ يُدْخِلُني الجَنَّةَ، ويُبَاعِدُني عن النَّارِ؟ قَالَ: « لَقَدْ سَأَلْتَ عن عَظِيمٍ، وإنَّهُ لَيَسِيرٌ عَلى مِنْ يَسَّرَهُ اللَّه تَعَالى علَيْهِ: تَعْبُدُ اللَّهَ لا تُشْرِكُ بِهِ شيْئاً، وتُقِيمُ الصَّلاةَ، وتُؤتِي الزَّكاةَ، وتصُومُ رمضَانَ وتَحُجُّ البيْتَ إن استطعت إلَيْهِ سبِيلاً » ثُمَّ قَالَ: « ألا أدُلُّكَ عَلى أبْوابِ الخيْرِ؟ الصَّوْمُ جُنَّةٌ، الصَّدَقَةُ تُطْفِئُ الخطيئةَ كما يُطْفِئُ الماءُ النَّارَ، وصلاةُ الرَّجُلِ مِنْ جوْفِ اللَّيلِ » ثُمَّ تَلا: ﴿ تتجافى جُنُوبُهُمْ عَنِ المَضَاجِعِ ﴾ حتَّى بلَغَ ﴿ يَعْمَلُونَ ﴾ [السجدة: 16]. ثُمَّ قال: « ألا أخْبِرُكَ بِرَأْسِ الأمْرِ، وعمودِهِ، وذِرْوةِ سَنامِهِ؟» قَالَ: « رَأْسُ الأمْرِ الإسْلامُ، وعَمُودُهُ الصَّلاةُ. وذروةُ سنامِهِ الجِهَادُ » ثُمَّ قال: « ألا أخْبِرُكَ بِمِلاكِ ذلكَ كله؟» قُلْتُ : بَلى يا رسُولَ اللَّهِ! فَأَخَذَ بِلسانِهِ قال: « كُفَّ علَيْكَ هذا » قُلْتُ: يا رسُولَ اللَّهِ، وإنَّا لمُؤَاخَذون بِما نَتَكلَّمُ بِهِ؟ فقال: ثَكِلتْكَ أُمُّكَ، وهَلْ يَكُبُّ النَّاسَ في النَّارِ على وَجُوهِهِم إلاَّ حصَائِدُ ألْسِنتِهِم؟ ». رواه الترمذي وقال: حدِيثٌ حسَنٌ صحِيحٌ.

"I said to the Messenger of Allah ﷺ: 'Inform me of an act which will cause me to enter Jannah and keep me far from Hell?' He replied: 'You have asked me about a matter of great importance, but it is easy for one for whom Allah makes it easy.' He added, 'Worship Allah, associate nothing with Him in worship, offer As-Salaat (the prayer), pay the Zakaat, observe Saum (fasting) during Ramadaan and perform the Hajj (pilgrimage) to the House of Allah if you can afford it.' He further said, 'Shall I not guide you to the gates of goodness? Fasting is a screen (from Hell), charity extinguishes the sins as water extinguishes fire, and standing in prayer by a slave of Allah during the last third of the night.' Then he recited: **"Their sides forsake their beds, to invoke their Lord in fear and hope, and they spend (in charity in Allah's Cause) out of what We have bestowed on them. No person knows what is kept hidden for them of joy**

as a reward for what they used to do." (As-Sajdah, 17-18)
Then he added: 'Shall I tell you of the root of the matter, its
pillar and its highest point?' I replied: 'Yes! Certainly, O
Messenger of Allah!' He said: 'The root of the matter
(foundation) is Islam, its pillars (mainstay is) As-Salaat (the
prayer) and its highest point is Jihaad (to fight in the cause of
Allah).' Then he (ﷺ) asked: 'Shall I tell you of that which holds
all these things?' I said: 'Yes, O Messenger of Allah!' So He took
hold of his tongue and said: 'Keep this in control.' I asked: 'O
Messenger of Allah! Shall we really be accounted for what we
talk about?' He replied: 'May your mother lose you! Will people
will be thrown on their faces into the Hellfire for other than on
account of their tongues?!" [At-Tirmidhi]

[EXPLANATION OF HADITHS 1516 TO 1522]

The author mentions these narrations to highlight and warn about the evils and severity of the tongue; an individual may utter a word thoughtlessly, paying no attention to what he says, and by it he obtains the displeasure of Allah ﷻ. So safeguard your tongue from uttering the wrong thing, for certainly, uttering the wrong word is a means to many trials and tribulations! Without doubt, many calamities originate from the utterance of the tongue. For example: many people, without even knowing it, supplicate against themselves and perceive it not, or against their offspring, friends, relatives, etc. and there is a possibility that the door for supplications to be accepted may be open during that time and the supplication is answered!

In the narration of Mu'adh ibn Jabal ﷺ, the Prophet ﷺ said to him: "Shall I tell you of that which holds all these things?" Meaning: that thing which keeps these aforementioned things altogether? So Mu'adh said: "Yes, O Messenger of Allah!" So the Messenger of Allah ﷺ took hold of his tongue and said: "Keep this in control." Mu'adh then asked: "O Messenger of Allah! Shall we really be accounted for what we talk about?" to which the Prophet ﷺ replied: "May your mother lose you!" And this statement of the Prophet ﷺ was frequently used by him, and why the Prophet ﷺ would utter these words would be to indicate and point out something very important (and not that he actually meant it literally). And then the Prophet ﷺ said: "Will people will be thrown on their faces into the Hellfire for other than on account of their tongues?!'"

So my brothers (and sisters)! Beware of the dangers of your tongues and safeguard them! This is achieved by preventing them from lying, cheating, giving false testimony, slandering others, backbiting, and every statement which distances one away from Allah ﷻ, as well as whatever statement leads to Allah's punishment. Distance yourselves from these things! We ask Allah the Exalted for us and for you, to protect and safeguard us upon the Deen; indeed He has the ability to do so!

[Hadith 1523]

Abu Hurairah said: the Messenger of Allah ﷺ said:

« أَتَدْرُونَ ما الغِيبَةُ؟» قَالُوا : اللهُ ورسُولُهُ أَعْلَمُ. قال : « ذِكْرُكَ أَخاكَ بِما يَكْرَهُ » قِيل : أَفَرَأَيْتَ إِنْ كان

في أَخِي ما أَقُولُ؟ قَالَ : « إِنْ كانَ فِيهِ ما تَقُولُ فَقَدِ اغْتَبْتَهُ ، وإِنْ لَمْ يَكُنْ فِيهِ ما تَقُولُ فَقَدْ بَهَتَّهُ » رواه

مسلم .

"Do you know what backbiting is?" The companions said: "Allah and His Messenger know better." Thereupon he said: "Backbiting is talking about your (Muslim) brother in a manner he dislikes." It was said to Him: "What if my (Muslim) brother is as I say?" He said: "If he is actually as you say, then that is backbiting; but if that is not in him, that is slandering." [Muslim]

[Hadith 1524]

Abu Bakrah ﷺ said: the Messenger of the Allah ﷺ said, while delivering the sermon during the Farewell Pilgrimage on the Day of Sacrifice at Mina:

« إِنَّ دِماءَكُم ، وأَمْوالَكُم وأَعْراضَكُم حرامٌ عَلَيْكُم كَحُرْمة يومِكُم هذا ، في شهرِكُمْ هذا ، في بَلَدِكُم هذا ،

أَلا هَلْ بَلَّغْت » متفقٌ عليه .

"Verily your blood, your property and your honour are as sacred and inviolable just as the sanctity of this day of yours, in this month of yours and in this town of yours. Verily! I have conveyed this message to you." [Agreed Upon]

[Hadith 1525]

A'ishah ﷺ said:

وعنْ عائِشة رضِي اللهُ عنْها قَالَتْ : قُلْتُ للنبِي صَلَّى اللهُ عَلَيْهِ وسَلَّم حسبُكَ مِنْ صفِيَّة كذا وكَذَا قال

بعْضُ الرُّواةِ : تعْني قَصِيرةٌ ، فقال : « لَقَدْ قُلْتِ كَلِمةً لو مُزِجتْ بماءِ البحْرِ لمزَجتْهُ ، » قَالَتْ : وحكَيْتُ

له إنساناً فقال : « ما أُحِبُّ أَنِي حكَيْتُ إِنْساناً وإِنَّ لي كذا وَكَذَا » رواه أبو داود ، والترمذي وقال :

حديثٌ حسنٌ صحيحٌ .

"I said to the Prophet: 'Such-and-such thing of Safiyyah is sufficient for you.' (She meant Safiyyah was a short woman). He said: 'You have indeed uttered a word which would pollute the sea if it were mixed in it.'" She further said: "I imitated a person before the Prophet ﷺ and he said: 'I do not like that I should imitate someone even (if I am paid) in return for such-and-such." [Abu Dawud and At-Tirmidhi]

[Hadith 1526]

Anas ﷺ said: the Messenger of Allah ﷺ said:

« لَمَّا عُرِجَ بِي مَرَرْتُ بِقَوْمٍ لَهُمْ أَظْفَارٌ مِنْ نُحَاسٍ يَخْمِشُونَ بِهَا وُجُوهَهُمْ وَصُدُورَهُمْ، فَقُلْتُ: مَنْ هؤُلَاءِ يَا جِبْرِيلُ؟ قَالَ: هؤُلَاءِ الَّذِينَ يَأْكُلُونَ لُحُومَ النَّاسِ، وَيَقَعُونَ فِي أَعْرَاضِهِمْ » رواهُ أبو داود.

"During the Miraaj (the Night Ascension), I saw a group of people who were scratching their faces with copper nails. I asked: 'Who are these people, O Jibril?' Jibril replied: 'These are the people who ate the flesh of others (by backbiting) and trampled on people's honour." [Abu Dawud]

[Hadith 1527]

Abu Hurairah reported the Messenger of Allah said:

« كُلُّ المُسْلِمِ عَلَى المُسْلِمِ حَرَامٌ : دَمُهُ وعِرْضُهُ وَمَالُهُ » رواهُ مسلم .

"The blood, honour and property of a Muslim are inviolable to another Muslim." [Muslim]

[EXPLANATION OF HADITHS 1523 TO 1527]

The author mentions these remaining narrations regarding backbiting, and they point to a number of things: they highlight and clarify the matter pertaining to backbiting, that is, saying about your brother (or sister) that which they dislike. In brief we will say that this could be in regards to one's Deen, manners, physical appearance, his family and so on. Also we said, if one does says something about an individual behind his back while advising someone for a good reason then this is allowed.

Regarding the narration of Abu Bakrah ﷺ, the Prophet ﷺ clarified the unlawfulness of a person's blood, wealth and honour, and he delivered this speech wherein he mentioned these things in his farewell speech, when masses of his companions had gathered, about a hundred thousand of them. The Prophet ﷺ addressed them saying: "Verily your blood, your property and your honour are as sacred and inviolable just as the sanctity of this day of yours, in this month of yours and in this town of yours. Verily! I have conveyed this message to you."

The remaining narrations also indicate the impermissibility of saying something about your brother which he dislikes, and this could be regarding his physical appearance - such as his height, whether he is tall or short, etc. The likes of this is forbidden and the Hadith of A'ishah ﷺ indicates that for she uttered statements about Safiyyah ﷺ, who was one of the *Mothers of the Believers*, and was corrected by the Prophet ﷺ. A'ishah ﷺ said about her: "Such-and-such thing of Safiyyah is sufficient for you." And what she meant was that Safiyyah ﷺ

was a short person. The Prophet ﷺ said to her in response: "You have indeed uttered a word which would pollute the sea if it were mixed in it." What the Prophet ﷺ meant was, these few words, which had been given little importance by A'ishah ﵂, due to their severity, would affect this sea even though it is so large and wide. It is possible that these words A'ishah ﵂ uttered could have made the Prophet ﷺ dislike Safiyyah ﵂ in some way, which would have certainly affected her.

Regarding the narration about the Miraaj (the Night Ascension), whatever the case may be, it is an obligation upon everyone to control his or her tongue and to utter only that which is good if they have faith in Allah and the last Day as the Prophet ﷺ said: "He who believes in Allah and the Last Day must either speak good or remain silent."

So we ask Allah to protect us and you from His displeasure and to aid and help us to be grateful to Him and in perfecting (our) devotion towards Him!

[Chapter] The Prohibition Of Listening To Backbiting

Allah the Exalted says in the Qur'an:

وَإِذَا سَمِعُوا۟ ٱللَّغْوَ أَعْرَضُوا۟

"And when they hear Al-Laghw (dirty, false, evil vain talk), they withdraw from it." (Al-Qasas, 55)

Allah the Exalted also says:

وَٱلَّذِينَ هُمْ عَنِ ٱللَّغْوِ مُعْرِضُونَ

"And those who turn away from Al-Laghw (dirty, false, evil vain talk, falsehood, and all that Allah has forbidden)." (Al-Mu'minoon, 3)

Allah also says:

إِنَّ ٱلسَّمْعَ وَٱلْبَصَرَ وَٱلْفُؤَادَ كُلُّ أُو۟لَـٰٓئِكَ كَانَ عَنْهُ مَسْـُٔولًا

"The hearing, and the sight, and the heart, of each of those you will be questioned." (Al-Isra', 36)

The Exalted also says:

وَإِذَا رَأَيْتَ ٱلَّذِينَ يَخُوضُونَ فِىٓ ءَايَـٰتِنَا فَأَعْرِضْ عَنْهُمْ حَتَّىٰ يَخُوضُوا۟ فِى حَدِيثٍ غَيْرِهِۦ ۚ وَإِمَّا يُنسِيَنَّكَ ٱلشَّيْطَـٰنُ فَلَا تَقْعُدْ بَعْدَ ٱلذِّكْرَىٰ مَعَ ٱلْقَوْمِ ٱلظَّـٰلِمِينَ

"And when you (O Muhammad) see those who engage in a false conversation about Our verses (of the Qur'an), stay away from them till they turn to another topic. And if Satan causes you to forget, then after the remembrance sit not you in the company of those people who are the polytheists and wrong doings." (Al-An'aam, 68)

[Hadith 1528]

Reported by Abu ad-Darda ﷺ: the Prophet ﷺ said:

« مَنْ رَدَّ عَنْ عِرْضِ أخيهِ، رَدَّ اللهُ عنْ وجْهِهِ النَّارَ يوْمَ القِيَامَةِ » رواه الترمذي وقالَ: حديثٌ حسنٌ.

"He who defends the honour of his (Muslim) brother, Allah will secure his face against the Fire on the Day of Resurrection." [At-Tirmidhi]

[Hadith 1529]

Itbaan ibn Maalik ﷺ said in a long Hadith cited in the Chapter entitled "Hope":

« أيْنَ مالِكُ بنُ الدُّخْشُمِ ؟ » فَقَال رجل: ذلكَ مُنافِقٌ لا يُحِبُّ اللهَ ورسُولَهُ ، فَقَالَ النبي صَلَّى اللهُ عَلَيْهِ وسَلَّم : « لا تقُلْ ذلكَ ، ألا تَراه قد قَال : لا إلَهَ إلاَّ اللهُ يُريدُ بذلكَ وجْهَ اللهِ ، وإن اللهَ قدْ حَرَّمَ على النَّارِ منْ قال : لا إله إلاَّ اللهُ يبْتَغِي بِذلكَ وجْهَة اللهِ » متفقٌ عليه .

"When the Prophet stood to offer As-Salaat (the prayer) he asked: 'Where is Maalik ibn Ad-Dukhshum?' A man replied: 'He is a hypocrite. He does not love Allah and His Messenger.' The Prophet ﷺ said: 'Do not say that. Do you not know that he said: "La ilaha illallah (there is no true god except Allah)" seeking His pleasure? Allah has made the Fire of Hell unlawful for him who affirms that none has the right to be worshipped but Allah.'" [Agreed Upon]

[EXPLANATION OF CHAPTER: THE PROHIBITION OF LISTENING TO BACKBITING AND HADITHS 1528 AND 1529]

The author (Imam An-Nawawi) mentioned numerous evidences pointing out the seriousness of backbiting, its evils, harms and impact, and he ends this chapter with many evidences pointing out the ruling regarding listening to backbiting. We say, one has been completely forbidden to listen to any types of backbiting, and one has been commanded in this case, to divert such gatherings to another subject if one hears any backbiting in them. In doing so, one will obtain immense reward and this is what the Hadith of Abu ad-Darda' indicates. If one happens to be in a gathering when backbiting occurs and is unable to change the subject, it becomes a must upon him to get up and leave that gathering immediately, as Allah's says in the Qur'an:

وَقَدْ نَزَّلَ عَلَيْكُمْ فِى ٱلْكِتَٰبِ أَنْ إِذَا سَمِعْتُمْ ءَايَٰتِ ٱللَّهِ يُكْفَرُ بِهَا وَيُسْتَهْزَأُ بِهَا فَلَا تَقْعُدُوا۟ مَعَهُمْ حَتَّىٰ يَخُوضُوا۟ فِى حَدِيثٍ غَيْرِهِۦٓ إِنَّكُمْ إِذًا مِّثْلُهُمْ إِنَّ ٱللَّهَ جَامِعُ ٱلْمُنَٰفِقِينَ وَٱلْكَٰفِرِينَ فِى جَهَنَّمَ جَمِيعًا

"And it has already been revealed to you in the Book (this Qur'an) that when you hear the verses of Allah being denied and mocked at, then sit not with them, until they engage in a talk other than that; (if you stay with them) certainly in that case you would be would be like them." (An-Nisaa', 140)

So this verse clearly indicates that if a person happens to be among a group of people who are engaging in backbiting, and he remains there listening to them backbiting, that individual shares in that sin for merely listening and not leaving.

The author mentions a number of verses regarding turning away from idle, indecent speech. The word "Al-Laghw" refers to any speech one utters that has no benefit in it. The servants of the Most-Merciful Allah are described in the Qur'an as:

$$وَالَّذِينَ لَا يَشْهَدُونَ الزُّورَ وَإِذَا مَرُّوا بِاللَّغْوِ مَرُّوا كِرَامًا$$

"And if they pass by some evil play or evil talk, they pass by it with dignity." (Al-Furqaan, 72)

This means, they are not affected by it, they do not pay any heed to it or listen to it.

The author also mentions a narration of Itbaan ibn Maalik regarding Maalik ibn Ad-Dukhshum ﷺ, when an individual spoke regarding his honour in the presentence of the Prophet ﷺ. The Prophet ﷺ forbid this individual from doing so and said:

$$أَلَا تَرَاهُ قد قَالَ : لَا إِلَهَ إِلَّا اللهُ يُرِيدُ بِذلِك وجه الله$$

"Do you not know that he said: 'La ilaha illallah (there is no true god except Allah)' seeking His pleasure?"

So this is proof that if a person says similar statements and the person is not so, this counts as backbiting him, but on the other hand, backbiting a disbeliever is not the same, and it is allowed to backbite any disbeliever, but if he has Muslim relatives then one should not backbite him. And as for the sinful Muslim, then we have been forbidden to backbite him unless there is a genuine benefit in doing so, in which case it would be allowed to advise someone regarding them. And Allah grants success!

[Hadith 1530]

Ka'b ibn Maalik ﷺ said in his long story about his repentance:

قَالَ النَّبِيُّ ﷺ وهُوَ جَالِسٌ في القَوْمِ بِتَبُوكَ : « مَا فَعَلَ كَعْبُ بنُ مَالِكٍ ؟ » فقَالَ رَجُلٌ مِنْ بَني سلِمَةَ : يَا رسُولَ اللهِ حبسهُ بُرْداهُ ، والنَّظَرُ في عِطْفَيْهِ . فقَالَ لَهُ مُعاذُ بنُ جبلٍ رضي اللهُ عنه : بِئْسَ ما قُلْتَ ، واللهِ يَا رسُولَ اللهِ مَا عَلِمْنا عليْهِ إلاَّ خيْراً ، فَسكَتَ رسُولُ اللهِ ﷺ .متفق عليه .

"The Prophet ﷺ was sitting among the people in Tabuk. He said: 'What happened to Ka'b ibn Maalik?' A person from the tribe of Banu Salamah said: 'O Messenger of Allah! He has been stopped by his two cloaks and his looking at his own flanks with pride!' Murad ibn Jabil said: 'Woe be to you! You have passed an indecent remark. O Messenger of Allah! By Allah, we know nothing about him but good!' The Messenger of Allah remained silent." [Agreed Upon]

[EXPLANATION OF HADITH 1530]

Imam An-Nawawi ﷺ mentions this narration related to the story regarding Ka'b and two others who refrained from going to the battle of Tabuk without a valid reason, and they were Maraar ibn Rabi and Hilaal ibn Umayah. Upon the Prophet's ﷺ return from the expedition, those who refrained without valid reasons would present themselves to the Prophet ﷺ putting forth to him idle excuses as to why they had not gone to the battle. So the Prophet ﷺ accepted those that gave him excuses on face value and left their hidden intent to Allah, but these three who never left to this battle spoke nothing but the absolute truth. They refrained from this expedition without a valid excuse. So the Prophet ﷺ ordered that none talk with them and to forsake them, to the point that when they would greet anyone, no one would return the greetings. And it was the case that Ka'b would greet the Prophet ﷺ and he would not know whether or not the Prophet's ﷺ lips would even move in replying to Ka'b's greetings.

After 48 days, the Prophet ﷺ ordered the three men's wives to dissociate themselves with their husbands, and these women companions were meant to go to their families' homes. The wives of Hilaal ibn Umayah and Maraar ibn Rabi, after the Prophet ﷺ commanded the wives to separate, explained to the Prophet ﷺ that their husbands were in great need of them, so the Prophet ﷺ gave these two men a special allowance for their wives to tend to them. But as for Ka'b, then his wife was commanded by the Prophet ﷺ to go to her family's home.

This story is for sure, a great magnificent event that happened, and in which Allah ﷺ revealed verses regarding it from the Qur'an. And reading (this story, or any other story in the Qur'an) one acquires for every letter ten good deeds, meaning it is equal to ten virtuous good deeds. Allah Exalted be He, says in the Qur'an about these three who remained behind from this battle:

وَعَلَى ٱلثَّلَٰثَةِ ٱلَّذِينَ خُلِّفُواْ حَتَّىٰٓ إِذَا ضَاقَتْ عَلَيْهِمُ ٱلْأَرْضُ بِمَا رَحُبَتْ وَضَاقَتْ عَلَيْهِمْ أَنفُسُهُمْ وَظَنُّوٓاْ أَن لَّا مَلْجَأَ مِنَ ٱللَّهِ إِلَّآ إِلَيْهِ ثُمَّ تَابَ عَلَيْهِمْ لِيَتُوبُوٓاْ إِنَّ ٱللَّهَ هُوَ ٱلتَّوَّابُ ٱلرَّحِيمُ

"And (He did forgive also) the three [who did not join the Tabuk expedition (whom the Prophet ﷺ)] left (i.e. He did not give judgment in their case, suspended for Allah's Decision) till for them the earth, vast as it is, was straitened on them and their own selves were straitened to them, and they perceived that there is no fleeing from Allah, and no refuge but with Him. Then, He accepted their repentance, that they might repent (unto Him). Verily, Allah is the One who accepts repentance, Most Merciful." (At-Tawbah, 118)

So during this expedition while the Prophet ﷺ was sitting, he asked about Ka'b, so a man from those present said: "O Messenger of Allah! The embellishment of his cloak an appreciation of his sides have allured him, and he was thus detained." So no doubt this type speech is backbiting, as Ka'b would surely have been displeased to hear that. Allah the Exalted allowed for Ka'b to be defended (by another companion), and so Mu'adh ibn Jabal replied: "We know nothing about him but good." To which the Messenger of Allah ﷺ remained silent. And what is to be benefited from this is, if an individual happens to be backbitten in one's presence, it become obligatory upon those present to defend that individual being backbitten, by either saying to the backbiter: "Be quiet!" Or by saying: "Fear Allah!" Or one can advise this individual to stop backbiting in the most notable manner, and if this is not possible, then one must separate oneself from these places where such backbiting occurs.

In short, if one sits in any gathering in which the righteous and good doers are backbitten, it is an obligation upon the listener to defend the backbitten and if this is not possible, one must leave, and if the person does neither, and remains in that gather, he will share in the sin as well. And Allah grants success!

[Chapter] Some Cases Where It Is Permissible To Backbite

Backbiting is permissible only for valid reasons approved by the Shariah. These reasons are as follows:

1. It is permissible for an oppressed person to speak before a judge or someone in a similar position of authority to help him establish his or her rights by telling him "so-and-so wronged me and has done such-and-such to me", etc.

2. It is permissible to seek somebody's assistance in forbidding evil and helping someone change his or her immoral conduct. One can say to the person who can offer such assistance, "so-and-so does such-and-such evil deeds. Can you exhort him?" etc. This is permissible as long as one intends to forbid evil. If however, one intends something else apart from this, then this act becomes unlawful.

3. One who seeks a legal verdict on a certain matter may point out the default of another person or relate something else. In this case one can say to the Mufti: "My father or my brother (for example) treated me unjustly." etc. This is permissible to say only if need be, but it is better to say: "What do you think of someone who did such-and-such?" This does not mean however, that naming the person in question is not permissible; Hadith Number 1532 makes this point clear.

4. One who criticizes those who openly commit acts of disobedience, such as drinking wine, gambling, engaging in immoral habits, fornication, hypocrisy, and making mischief.

5. It is permissible to call into question the narrators of Hadith, and witness in the court when the need arises. It is also permissible to mention the bad qualities of somebody for marriage purpose in case an advice is sought. Also, if one has noticed that a seeker of knowledge frequents the gatherings of an innovator in religion and one fears that this person may be affected by this so-called scholar, then he must in this case give counsel to the seeker of knowledge by telling him about the innovator, etc.

6. It is permissible to use names such as "Al-A'mash" (which means "the blear-eyed") to talk about people who are known by such names for the sake of identification and not for disparaging people and underestimating them. To identify them without resorting to such names is however better.

[Hadith 1531]

A'ishah ⁓ said: a man sought permission for an audience with the Prophet ⁓ so he said:

« ائْذَنُوا لهُ، بئسَ أخو العشِيرَةِ » متفقٌ عليه .

"Give him permission but he is a bad member of his tribe."
[Agreed Upon]

[Hadith 1532]

A'ishah ﷺ said: the Messenger of Allah ﷺ said:

« مَا أَظُنُّ فُلاناً وفُلاناً يعرِفَانِ مِنْ دِينِنَا شَيْئاً » رواه البخاريُّ. قال الليثُ بنُ سعْدٍ أحدُ رُواةِ هذا الحَدِيثِ: هذَانِ الرَّجُلانِ كَانَا مِنَ المُنَافِقِينَ.

"I do not think that so-and-so understands anything of our faith." [Al-Bukhari; Al-Laith ibn Sa'd, who is one of the narrators of this Hadith, said: "the two men mentioned by the Prophet ﷺ in this Hadith were hypocrites"]

[Hadith 1533]

Fatimah bint Qais ﷺ said: I came to the Prophet ﷺ and said to him: "Mu'awiyah ibn Abi Sufyaan and Abu Jahm sent me a proposal of marriage." The Messenger of Allah ﷺ said:

« أَمَّا مُعَاوِيَةُ ، فَصُعْلُوكٌ لا مالَ لهُ ، وأَمَّا أَبو الجَهْمِ فلا يضَعُ العَصا عن عَاتِقِهِ » متفقٌ عليه.

"As for Mu'awiyah he is poor and he has no property, and as for Abu Jahm, his stick never leaves his side (he beats women)." [Agreed Upon]

[Hadith 1534]

Zaid ibn Al-Arqam ﷺ said:

خَرجْنَا مع رسولِ اللهِ ﷺ في صابٍ في النَّاسِ فيهِ شِدَّةٌ، فقال عبدُ اللهِ بنُ أُبَيٍّ: لا تُنْفِقُوا على مِنْ عِنْدِ رسُولِ اللهِ ﷺ حتى يَنْفَضُّوا وقال: لَئِنْ رجَعْنَا إلى المدينةِ لَيُخْرِجَنَّ الأعَزُّ مِنْها الأذَلَّ، فَأَتَيْتُ رسولَ اللهِ ﷺ، فَأَخْبَرْتُهُ بِذلكَ، فَأَرسَلَ إلى عبدِ اللهِ بنِ أُبَيٍّ فَاجْتَهَدَ يمِينَهُ: ما فَعَ، فقالوا: كَذَبَ زيدٌ رسولَ اللهِ ﷺ، فَوَقَعَ في نَفْسِي مِمَّا قالوا شِدَّةٌ حتى أنْزَلَ اللهُ تعالى تَصْدِيقِي: ﴿ إِذَا جَاءَكَ المُنَافِقُونَ ﴾ ثم دعاهم النبيُّ ﷺ، لِيَسْتغْفِرَ لهم فلَوَّوْا رُؤُوسَهُمْ. متفقٌ عليه.

"We set out on a journey along with the Messenger of Allah ﷺ and we faced many hardships. Abdullah ibn Ubayd (the chief of the hypocrites at Al-Madinah) said to his friend: "'Do not spend on those who are with the Messenger Allah till those who are with him desert him.' He also said: 'If we return to Al-Madinah, the more honourable (meaning himself, i.e., Abdullah ibn Ubayd) will drive out there from the meaner (meaning, the Messenger of Allah ﷺ)." I went to the Messenger of Allah to inform him about that and he sent someone to Abdullah ibn Ubayd. He asked him whether he had said that or not. Abdullah took an oath that he had not done anything of the sort and said that it was Zaid who carried a false tale to the Messenger of Allah ﷺ." Zaid said: "I was so much perturbed because of this until this verse was revealed (from the Qur'an) verifying my statement: **'When the hypocrites come to you (O Muhammad), they say: "We bear witness that you are indeed the Messenger of Allah, and Allah knows that you are indeed His Messenger, and Allah bears witness that the hypocrites are lairs.'** (Al-Munaafiqoon, 1) Then the Messenger of Allah ﷺ called the hypocrites in order to seek forgiveness for them from Allah, but they turned away their heads." [Agreed Upon]

[EXPLANATION OF HADITHS 1531 TO 1534]

Imam An-Nawawi 🙵 mentions in this chapter what is permissible from backbiting, and he mentions a few narrations indicating this and from them is the statement of A'ishah 🙵 who reported that a man sought the permission to enter upon the Prophet 🙵, meaning to go into the Prophet's house, so the Prophet 🙵 said: "Give him permission but he is a bad member of his tribe." And another narration: "He is a bad brother of his tribe." Regarding this individual, then he was a person known to be from those who were from the people of corruption and error, so this narration points out the permissibility to backbite such people who are in error and are corrupt within themselves.

But why is allowance given to backbite them? The reason why is to alert the people about those individuals and their misguidance, to let their corrupt and sinful ways be known so that those who are unaware of their deceptive behaviour will be on guard from such misguidance and not easily charmed or fascinated by them. Such individuals can easy deceive the masses and lead them to think that they are upon good when in fact this is quite the opposite. In this circumstance it becomes an obligation on whosoever knows this corrupt person's circumstance to make that known to the people and that is by saying to them, "this individual is upon such-and-such," or "this person, there is no good in him."

And how many people are eloquent with their tongues, well-spoken and looked upon as righteous due to their appearance but in actual fact, there is no good in them whatsoever! So such deceiving people should be exposed, like we said, for the general benefit of the public.

A'ishah ﷺ further reports the Prophet ﷺ said:

« مَا أَظُنُّ فُلاناً وفُلاناً يعرِفَانِ مِنْ دِينِنا شَيْئاً »

"I do not think that so-and-so and so-and-so understand anything of our faith."

So regarding these individuals the Prophet ﷺ was referring to, then they were two hypocrites, and so the Prophet ﷺ made apparent their condition, which was evil, and that was by saying they did not understand anything from the Deen of Islam, as the hypocrite lacks true understanding of Allah's Religion and their hearts are far and distant from it. We seek refuge in Allah from this! One of the traits of the hypocrites is to manifest Emaan and at the same time hide their Kufr as Allah ﷻ says regarding them in the Qur'an:

وَمِنَ ٱلنَّاسِ مَن يَقُولُ ءَامَنَّا بِٱللَّهِ وَبِٱلْيَوْمِ ٱلْأَخِرِ وَمَا هُم بِمُؤْمِنِينَ ۞ يُخَٰدِعُونَ ٱللَّهَ وَٱلَّذِينَ ءَامَنُوا۟ وَمَا يَخْدَعُونَ إِلَّآ أَنفُسَهُمْ وَمَا يَشْعُرُونَ

"And of mankind, there are some (hypocrites) who say: 'We believe in Allah and in the Last Day' while in fact they believe not, they (think to) deceive Allah those who believe, while they only deceive themselves, and perceive (it) not." (Al-Baqarah, 8-9)

The author next mentions the narration of Fatimah Bint Qais ﷺ in which she sought the Prophet's ﷺ legal opinion regarding three individuals seeking her hand in marriage and they were Mu'awiyah ibn Abi Sufyaan, Abu Jahm and Usamah ibn Zaid. The Prophet said to her: "As for Mu'awiyah he is poor and he has no property." Sometime after this event, Mu'awiyah became the Khalifah of the Muslims, his financially condition changed and improved greatly.

The Prophet ﷺ said: "As for Mu'awiyah he is poor and he has no property, and as for Abu Jahm, his stick never leaves his side (he beats women)." As for Abu Jahm, some interpret this to mean he was always travelling or always on a journey, because it is known that those who ride camels need to have a stick with them (to control the camel), but we say, it is to be interpreted as he hit women.

Some of the other narrations say the Prophet ﷺ said: "(Rather) marry Usamah ibn Zaid ibn Haarith." So Fatimah bint Qais married Usamah and in that there was great benefit. In summary, this Hadith we our explaining is a proof for the permissibility of mentioning someone's faults due to a valid reason, i.e. if someone comes to you asking your advice regarding an individual, the disclosure of that person's faults are allowed, and this is not counted as uncovering or exposing that individual's faults or disgracing them. There is a big difference between this and Al-Ghibah.

As for the fourth (and last Hadith), then it is narrated from Zaid ibn Al-Arqam ؓ who reports that the Prophet ﷺ was on one of his journeys and those who accompanied him included his companions as well as some of the hypocrites. As they were hard-pressed (due to lack of provisions), one of the hypocrites said:

$$\text{لَا تُنفِقُواْ عَلَىٰ مَنْ عِندَ رَسُولِ ٱللَّهِ حَتَّىٰ يَنفَضُّواْ}$$

"Spend not on those who are with Allah's Messenger until they desert Him." (Al-Munaafiqoon, 7)

And what this hypocrite meant was: do not spend on the companions of Prophet Muhammad ﷺ until they starve and eventually belie and abandon faith in the Prophet! But the true Believer in faith would never do such a thing, even if he or she is faced with death, hunger or thirst. Surely the true Believer will never forsake the Prophet Muhammad ﷺ.

But as it is known, this is the way the hypocrite thinks and this is one of their traits, i.e. they think the true believer, if he is given (something) he is pleased and if not, he is displeased (at his decree). But the devote believer does not behave this way. In short, their intent was not to merely make the companions leave the Prophet ﷺ, no, rather it was to make them disbelieve in him totally, as well as reject faith completely. The hypocrites also said:

لَإِن رَّجَعْنَآ إِلَى ٱلْمَدِينَةِ لَيُخْرِجَنَّ ٱلْأَعَزُّ مِنْهَا ٱلْأَذَلَّ

"If we return to Al-Madinah, indeed the more honourable (Abdullah ibn Ubayd) will expel therefrom the meaner (i.e. Allah's Messenger)." (Al-Munaafiqoon, 8)

Meaning: the most notable, greater and liked of his people will debase the lowly Prophet with humiliation. When Zaid ibn Al-Arqam ﷺ heard the hypocrite Abdullah ibn Ubayd say this, he went to the Prophet ﷺ and informed him about what had said. The Prophet ﷺ sent someone to affirm whether Abdullah had said these words, which he denied, and he also swore an oath. And for sure these are some of the ways, traits and manners of the hypocrites, that is, they take oaths knowing full well that they are lying and not telling the truth, and it was the habit of the Prophet ﷺ to leave what was concealed in their hearts (to Allah) and deal with them based upon what is apparent.

When Zaid got news that this hypocrite denied the allegation, Zaid become very worried over the matter, as this hypocrite swear by Allah and took a solemn oath that he had not said this and that Zaid was making this up and lying about him. The people started saying that Zaid was denying the Prophet ﷺ and that Zaid actually lied to him ﷺ, so Allah ﷻ revealed some verses affirming Zaid's truthfulness:

هُمُ ٱلَّذِينَ يَقُولُونَ لَا تُنفِقُوا عَلَىٰ مَنْ عِندَ رَسُولِ ٱللَّهِ حَتَّىٰ يَنفَضُّوا ۗ وَلِلَّهِ خَزَآئِنُ ٱلسَّمَٰوَٰتِ وَٱلْأَرْضِ وَلَٰكِنَّ ٱلْمُنَٰفِقِينَ لَا يَفْقَهُونَ • يَقُولُونَ لَئِن رَّجَعْنَآ إِلَى ٱلْمَدِينَةِ لَيُخْرِجَنَّ ٱلْأَعَزُّ مِنْهَا ٱلْأَذَلَّ ۚ وَلِلَّهِ ٱلْعِزَّةُ وَلِرَسُولِهِۦ وَلِلْمُؤْمِنِينَ وَلَٰكِنَّ ٱلْمُنَٰفِقِينَ لَا يَعْلَمُونَ

"They are the ones who say: 'Spend not on those who are with Allah's Messenger until they desert him.' And to Allah belongs the treasures of the heavens and the earth, but the hypocrites comprehend not. They (hypocrites) say: 'If we return to Al-Madinah, indeed the more honourable (Abdullah ibn Ubayd) will expel therefrom the meaner (i.e. Allah's Messenger);' but honour, power and glory belong to Allah, His Messenger (Muhammad) and to the believers, but the hypocrites know not." (Al-Munaafiqoon 7-8)

So look at how Allah answered Abdullah ibn Ubayd's statements! He the Exalted says: **"But honour, power and glory belong to Allah, His Messenger (Muhammad)."** Allah the Exalted never said that He is Alone honourable, no, for had He have said that, this would have given the hypocrites an indication and proof that they too have some honour. Rather Allah said: **"But honour, power and glory belong to Allah, His Messenger (Muhammad) and to the believers, but the hypocrites know not."**

So these verses are proof that an individual may relay to those in authority statements that the hypocrites utter, so as to take a stance regarding the corrupted sinful folk, and stop such statements from causing further corruption by spreading. This rule is general, and by this we mean, if an individual thinks that a person's statements may cause harm among the people he is allowed to raise that matter to those in authority or power, as doing so will be a preventative measure to eliminate this corruption being propagated amidst the masses. One should not be scared to raise such matters to those in authority assuming they may harm him for whatever reason, rather such an individual should not fear those in power or authority, as doing so and not bringing such a matter to them means this person is wronging himself (and the Muslims). A person should first be certain that the information he will convey to the authorities is correct, so as to not put himself under any hardship.

During the era of the Prophet ﷺ, when this matter occurred between Abdullah (the hypocrite) and Zaid, it was Revelation which came to the aid of Zaid. But in our time, that is not so and there is nothing to affirm a person's claims as well as to attest to his truthfulness, or expose the liar. This being this the case, one is obligated to refer such matters to those in authority to prevent corruption. Surely Allah grants success!

[Hadith 1535]

A'ishah ◌ said: Hind the wife of Abu Sufyaan, said to the Prophet ◌: Abu Sufyaan is a niggardly and does not give me and my daughter adequate provisions for maintenance unless I take from his possessions without him knowing. The Prophet ◌ said to her:

« خُذِي ما يكْفِيكِ ووَلَدَكِ بالمعْرُوفِ » متفقٌ عليه .

"Take from his possessions on a reasonable basis according to what may suffice you and your children." [Agreed Upon]

[EXPLANATION OF HADITH 1535]

Going overboard in spending is impermissible as well as denying those their rights such as the right to maintenance; if one is doing wrong regarding this, then it would be allowed and permitted for that individual's dependents to refer their matter to those in charge, so for this reason Hind went seeking the Prophet's ﷺ assistance.

One of the things we see in this narration is that the Prophet ﷺ did not rebuke her and say "such words you are uttering are forbidden" i.e. her husband was being niggardly. Rather he allowed her due to the fact that is was concerning her rights, so he said to her: "Take from his possessions on a reasonable basis according to what may suffice you and your children." So the Prophet ﷺ allowed her to take what was sufficient for her and her child without her husband's knowledge. This indicates the following:

1. The permissibility of backbiting the one who is oppressing and wronging you, but this has conditions, and one of them is that this person you refer the matter to can help you in that matter, but if this is not the case then one should not do that as it does not serve a purpose.

2. The obligation upon the husband to provide well for his family, his wife and offspring - even if his wife is wealthy as this makes no difference. And to add to this, we say if the wife is a teacher then he is not allowed to take any of her salary, not even a little, without her permission, especially if they both have agreed to her teaching and so forth, though he

124

provided her during here studies; so long as that was written in their marriage contract he has to stick to that agreement, so all her income belongs completely to her. But on the other hand, if they both agree that he will be entitled to some of that which she earns, then this is okay. For example, the husband states in their marriage contract, "I will allow you to work with the condition I will get half of your earnings or a third or fourth." This is okay based on what they both agree to.

3. The shows the permissibility for the one denied their due provisions to take from the one denying that maintenance without that individual's permission. So (for example) the wife may take from the husband's pocket, bag or his safe box what suffices her and her offspring.

If it is said: suppose an individual owes me money, but refuses to give it to me, would it be allowed for me to take what is owed to me without his permission? For example someone owes me 100 SR (Saudi Riyals), but this individual will not give me what he owes me, would I be allowed to take that amount by force from him? The answer to this is definitely no! It would not be allowed for you (or anyone else) to do this because there is a difference between this and person who is taking the wealth from the one who is supposed to be providing for you! So the reason is clearly apparent between the two and is backed up by the statement of the Prophet ﷺ when he said:

أَدِّ الأمانةَ إلى مَن ائْتَمَنَكَ وَلا تَخُنْ مَنْ خَانَكَ

"Pay the deposit to he who deposited it with you and (do) not betray (him) who betrayed you."

This is the preferred opinion regarding this issue, and some of the scholars have said, even if someone loans a person money and they refuse to give back that money, even in that case one is not allowed to take it back by force, and the proof they use is what we just mentioned to you: "And (do) not betray (him) who betrayed you." And Allah grants success!

[Chapter] The Prohibition of Talebearing

Allah the Exalted says in the Qur'an:

هَمَّازٍ مَّشَّاءٍ بِنَمِيمٍ

"A slanderer, going about with calumnies." (Al-Qalam, 11)

Also the Exalted says:

مَّا يَلْفِظُ مِن قَوْلٍ إِلَّا لَدَيْهِ رَقِيبٌ عَتِيدٌ

"Not a word does he (or she) utter but there is a watcher by him ready (to record it)." (Qaaf, 18)

[Hadith 1536]

Hudhaifah said: The Messenger of Allah said:

« لا يَدْخُلُ الجنةَ نَمَّامٌ» متفقٌ عليه .

"The person who goes about with calumnies will never enter Paradise." [Agreed Upon]

[Hadith 1537]

Ibn Abbas ﷺ said: The Messenger of Allah passed by two graves and said:

«إنَّهُمَا يُعَذَّبان ، وَمَا يُعَذَّبَانِ فِي كَبِيرٍ، بَلى إنَّهُ كَبِيرٌ : أمَّا أحَدُهُمَا ، فَكَانَ يَمشِي بِالنَّمِيمَةِ، وأمَّا الآخَرُ فَكَانَ لا يَسْتَتِرُ مِنْ بولِه » . متفقٌ عليه ، وهذا لفظ إحدى روايات البخاري .

"Both of them (the persons in these graves) are being tortured, and they are not being tortured for a major sin. But indeed they are great sins. One of them used not to save himself from being soiled with his urine, and the other one used to go about with calumnies (among the people to rouse hostilities)." [Al-Bukhari]

[Hadith 1538]

Ibn Mas'ud said: The Prophet said:

« ألا أُنبِّئُكم ما العَضْهُ ؟ هِي النَّمِيمَةُ ، القَالَةُ بَيْنَ النَّاسِ » رواه مسلم.

"Shall I tell you what Al-Adhu (falsehood and slander) is? It is talebearing which is committed among the people." [Muslim]

[EXPLANATION OF THE CHAPTER ON THE PROHIBITION OF TALEBEARING AND HADITHS 1536 TO 1538]

Regarding the previous section (i.e.) "Some cases where it is permissible to backbite," the author ﷺ mentioned six cases wherein backbiting is allowed, the first is when an individual is oppressed, so concession is given to him to seek help and assistance from the authorities, and the proof is the aforementioned Hadith of Hind. The meaning of Hind's words: "Abu Sufyaan is a niggardly" is that he was stingy and tight-fisted, so she described him like this to the Prophet ﷺ; but why? It is because she was being transgressed against and denied her God-given rights, so she wanted to know how she could obtain such rights and prevent harm being done to her. As is known, it is an obligation upon the husband to provide well for his wife and family, neither going too far in doing that nor falling short, rather he should maintain a medium course, as Allah ﷺ says in the Qur'an:

وَٱلَّذِينَ إِذَآ أَنفَقُواْ لَمْ يُسْرِفُواْ وَلَمْ يَقْتُرُواْ وَكَانَ بَيْنَ ذَٰلِكَ قَوَامًا

"And those, who, when they spend, are neither extravagant nor niggardly, but hold a medium (way) between those (extremes)." (Al-Furqaan, 67)

The author mentions in this chapter the Hadith of Ibn Mas'ud ﷺ, pertaining to the prohibition of calumny and talebearing, and the first thing we take from this narration is the astounding characteristic and method in which the Prophet ﷺ

taught the Muslims, and that was that by posing questions to those listening so as get their attention and make them fully alert to what he was going to inform them about. By this method, they would comprehend what the Prophet ﷺ was about to say and this would make them focused. So he asked: "Shall I tell you what Al-Adhu (falsehood and slander) is?" The Prophet ﷺ then said: "It is talebearing which is committed among the people." This means, a person spreads one person's words among others in order to create mischief in the ranks of the Muslims. Spreading people's words among others in order to create mischief is counted as one of the major sins. Hence when the Prophet ﷺ was shown two individuals being tortured in their graves, and he was informed as to why they were being tortured, one of them happened to spread slander and practise talebearing among the people.

And with regret there are those among us who constantly busy themselves day and night with these matters (slandering others) and we seek refuge with Allah from this! What these people do is, they go around saying to others: "So-and-so said such-and-such about you!" and similar statements, and either they are lying or they are being truthful, whatsoever the case may be, it is not allowed and both are counted as a major sin even if the person is, as we said, being truthful.

Allah the Exalted says regarding this in the Qur'an about obeying such types of individuals:

$$\text{وَلَا تُطِعْ كُلَّ حَلَّافٍ مَّهِينٍ • هَمَّازٍ مَّشَّآءٍ بِنَمِيمٍ}$$

"And obey not everyone who swears such, and is considered worthless, a slander, going about with calumnies." (Al-Qalam, 10-11)

So some of the people of knowledge have said regarding this verse that: "Whoever informs you that you have been slandered, know for sure he (himself the one who informs you) will also slander you." So what this means is, those who like going around informing others that they have been spoken ill of behind their back, some day or the other, they also will eventually slander and speak badly of you. So we say, if this becomes the case for you, pay no heed to those who inform you that others are going around slandering you.

This is proof indicating the Prophet's ﷺ unique, particular and remarkable way of conveying his message; he would spoke in such a way that it would attract one's attention instantly, and leave an individual completely focused on him and what he would be saying. And it goes without saying that he did this especially when he noticed those whom he would be addressing as heedless, inattentive and negligent. So it becomes a must upon you to take to this type of method the Prophet ﷺ always adopted, as for sure it will certainly help people to be able to memorize your words which you are conveying to them as well as help them also understand your speech better and grasp it fully, comprehend, absorb and digest.

If it is said: if an individual goes around making known what another individuals are upon, such as deceiving others, would it be allowed to transmit to others what this individual is doing? For example, the people are totally deceived by an individual, and due to this, a gullible individual confides with this person and tells him secrets and personal matters and befriends him, and then this deceiving individual makes known this person's secrets and personal matters to others.

Would it be allowed to notify the individual being deceived, that his personal affairs are being exposed to the masses? The answer is: Yes it would be allowed, and how that would be done is by saying to this person: "So-and-so, be careful of him, he is spreading among the people your business, secrets and your affairs." As you are informing this person this information, it is considered a form of general worthy advice, and this too does not fall under the type of matters that separate the people, as Allah says:

$$وَٱللَّهُ يَعْلَمُ ٱلْمُفْسِدَ مِنَ ٱلْمُصْلِحِ$$

"Allah knows him who means mischief from him who means good." (Al-Baqarah, 220)

And surely Allah grants success.

[Chapter] The Prohibition Of Carrying Tales and the People's Speech

Allah the Exalted says in the Qur'an:

وَلَا تَعَاوَنُواْ عَلَى ٱلْإِثْمِ وَٱلْعُدْوَٰنِ

"...Do not help one another in sin and transgression."
(Al-Maa'idah, 2)

In this chapter are similar Hadiths from the previous chapter.

[Hadith 1539]

Ibn Mas'ud ﷺ said: the Messenger of Allah ﷺ said:

«لا يُبَلِّغْني أحدٌ من أصْحابي عنْ أَحَدٍ شَيْئاً، فَإِنِّي أُحِبُّ أَنْ أَخْرُجَ إِلَيْكُمْ وأنا سليمُ الصَّدْرِ» رواه أبو داود والترمذي.

"None of My Companions should convey to me anything regarding another because I desire to meet every one of you with a clean heart. [Abu Dawud and At-Tirmidhi; Al-Albani graded this Hadith weak]

[EXPLANATION OF THE CHAPTER ON THE PROHIBITION OF CARRYING TALES AND THE PEOPLE'S SPEECH AND HADITH 1539]

The author (Imam An-Nawawi) ﷺ titles this chapter as the "Prohibition of carrying tales and the people's speech" and this should only be done with conditions, one of which is: if there is no benefit in an individual doing so, then one should not carry information. So the author's intent is that one should not expose the condition of another person if that does not serve a great purpose, for in doing so, it this leads to wronging that individual being exposed, and will also lead people to dislike this individual due to his faults being made known to them; many people think incorrectly, so hearing such information will only add to this.

Based upon this it is discouraged to relay information to the people, except if in doing so there is a great benefit or reason; that could be, if there is a fear that if they are not informed, that could lead to some type of corruption occurring or something similar. For example: if an individual speaks badly about those in authority in any of his sittings to others, in this case, this should not be brought to the attention of those in authority. Such as him saying, "They are like this" or, "They are like that," or he reviles them. In such a case, it would be preferred not to expose the words of this individual as this will lead that individual to fall in too many problems with them. But like we said, if not informing them of those who do these types of things will cause problems, corruption, etc. then it be would be allowed to inform them to prevent

134

harm coming to the people or to bring good or benefit. For example: we hear an individual speaking openly against the those in authority, exposing their sins or wrongdoings, etc. and spreading this among the people, in this case it would be highly encouraged to bring this to the attention of the authorities. And this would be counted as a type of advice so as to not let this individual persist and continue in his wrongdoing against them or attacking them, as this is recommended so as to prevent the masses from disliking those in office or power; leaving this individual free to commit further transgressions against them could lead to even more types of corruption being committed. For sure if people were left to speak as they wish and what they wish, much great wrongdoing would occur.

Regarding this matter, the author uses as proof a verse from the Qur'an and a narration, as for the verse, it is the statement of Allah :

وَلَا تَعَاوَنُوا عَلَى ٱلْإِثْمِ وَٱلْعُدْوَانِ

"...Do not help one another in sin and transgression." (Al-Maa'idah, 2)

And one of the things that is considered a sin and transgression is relating to spreading information about people or about a person without due reason or general benefit, and as we said in doing so, it leads to others hating and showing enmity toward the one that is mentioned to them without them having a valid Islamic reason.

And as for what is reported by Ibn Mas'ud, then it is the statement of the Prophet : "None of my companions should convey to me anything regarding another because I desire to meet every one of you with a clean heart." This narration indicates the wisdom of the Prophet ﷺ, and that was that he disliked knowing anything bad about anybody, whosoever that person was. And one of the reasons was so as to prevent and keep his heart free from having dislike for an individual due to what he might hear from another individual about him. And this is witnessed and occurs. How many of us know of a person who loved someone dearly and he was a person of sound faith and upright. Then this individual heard some information about his friend and straight away, he felt the strongest aversion towards this person and that made him flee away from him, as well as have hatred towards the one he had heard this information about.

In short, if there is a great need to inform others to prevent harm or stop corruption spreading, to decrease evil or stop it from prevailing, then then this is allowed (otherwise, it is not). And Allah grants success!

[Chapter] Ascertainment of What One Hears and Narrates

Allah ﷻ says in the Qur'an:

وَلَا تَقْفُ مَا لَيْسَ لَكَ بِهِ عِلْمٌ

"And follow not (O man, i.e., say not or do not or witness not) that which you have no knowledge." (Al-Isra', 36)

Also the Exalted says:

مَّا يَلْفِظُ مِن قَوْلٍ إِلَّا لَدَيْهِ رَقِيبٌ عَتِيدٌ

"Not a word does he (or she) utter, but there is a watcher by him ready (to record it)." (Al-Qaaf, 18)

[Hadith 1547]

Abu Hurairah ﷺ said: the Prophet ﷺ:

« كَفَى بِالمرءِ كَذِباً أَنْ يُحَدِّثَ بِكُلِّ ما سمِع » رواه مسلم .

"It is enough for a man to prove himself a liar when he goes on narrating whatever he hears." [Muslim]

[Hadith 1548]

Samurah ﷺ reported: The Messenger of Allah said:

« مَنْ حَدَّثَ عَنِّي بِحَدِيثٍ يَرَى أَنَّهُ كَذِبٌ ، فَهُو أَحدُ الكَاذِبِين » رواه مسلم .

"He who relates from me something which he deems false is one of two liars." [Muslim]

[Hadith 1549]

Asma' ﷺ reported: A woman came to the Messenger of Allah ﷺ and said: "I have a co-wife. Is there any harm for me if I give her the false impression of getting something from my husband which he has not in fact given me?" The Messenger of Allah ﷺ replied:

« الْمُتَشَبِّعُ بِمَا لَمْ يُعْطَ كَلَابِسِ ثَوْبَيْ زُورٍ » متفقٌ عليه .

"The one who creates a false impression of receiving what one has not been given is like one who wears two garments of falsehood." [Agreed Upon]

[EXPLANATION OF CHAPTER: ASCERTAINMENT OF WHAT ONE HEARS AND NARRATES AND HADITHS 1547 TO 1549]

We say regarding this chapter[1], it is upon the people to ascertain and verify information, whatever it is one hears. And this goes without saying in the time we are living in when mostly desires are followed and a majority of what people say is just gossip and idle talk. The author mentions proofs for this chapter, one of which is the statement of Allah ﷻ:

مَّا يَلْفِظُ مِن قَوْلٍ إِلَّا لَدَيْهِ رَقِيبٌ عَتِيدٌ

"And follow not (O man, i.e., say not or do not or witness not) that which you have no knowledge." (Al-Isra', 36)

"And follow not" means that an individual should not involve himself or delve into matters he has no knowledge of, and he should not utter words except that which he has knowledge pertaining to, as the Prophet ﷺ said: "He who believes in Allah and the Last Day must either speak good or remain silent."

مَّا يَلْفِظُ مِن قَوْلٍ إِلَّا لَدَيْهِ رَقِيبٌ عَتِيدٌ

"Not a word does he (or she) utter, but there is a watcher by him ready (to record it)." (Al-Qaaf, 18)

---

[1] This chapter follows on from some chapters related to lying. We have included it here because of its relevance to the subject of talebearing.

This means, there is a watcher over every individual, monitoring his (or her) every word. As for the word **"ready,"** it means the watcher over him never leaves that individual, so this is a warning for a person to be careful as to what he says without knowledge, as an individual doing so is sinful.

Next, the author mentions the narration of the Prophet ﷺ:

كفى بالمرء كذباً أنْ يُحَدِّثَ بكلِّ ما سمع

"It is enough for a man to prove himself a liar when he goes on narrating whatever he hears."

What this means is, if an individual talks and relates all what he hears without ascertaining that information, for sure he will be sooner or later be exposed and afflicted with lying. And this is a sure reality! Maybe someone comes to you saying "Such-and-such happened" but after investigation, it turns out that no such thing happened, or someone says to you, "So-and-so said such-and-such happened" and again, after investigation, it turns out that this person never said this!

And the worst things one can utter is regarding Allah's Religion, so one lies against Allah by explaining the Book of Allah based upon his own opinion and he explains it in a way other than how Allah wants it to be explained, or one lies against the Prophet ﷺ, and says, "The Prophet said such-and-such," and he is lying, or he knows full well it is something falsely attributed to the Prophet ﷺ but still insists on propagating it. If this is the case then this individual falls under the Hadith:

مَنْ حدَّث عنِّي بحَديثٍ يرَى أنَّهُ كذِبٌ ، فهُو أحدُ الكَاذِبين

"He who relates from me something which he deems false is one of two liars."

What is included in this regard, is lying regarding receiving something one did not receive, as occurred in the Hadith of Asma'. The reason why the woman wanted to do this, was to make her co-wife jealous of her and irritate her in spite of them being close and to spoil things between the co-wife and her husband. For this reason the Prophet ﷺ said:

المُتَشَبِّعُ بِما لم يُعْطَ كَلابِس ثَوْبَي زُورٍ

"The one who creates a false impression of receiving what one has not been given is like one who wears two garments of falsehood."

In short it is an obligation upon the Muslim to ascertain and verify any information he (or she) hears, whether he narrates it himself or what he hear from others; one has to consider whether the person who is informing him this information is truthful or not, as Allah the Exalted says:

يَٰٓأَيُّهَا ٱلَّذِينَ ءَامَنُوٓاْ إِن جَآءَكُمۡ فَاسِقُۢ بِنَبَإٍ فَتَبَيَّنُوٓاْ أَن تُصِيبُواْ قَوۡمَۢا

بِجَهَٰلَةٖ فَتُصۡبِحُواْ عَلَىٰ مَا فَعَلۡتُمۡ نَٰدِمِينَ

"O you who believe! If a rebellious evil person comes to you with news, verify it, lest you harm people in ignorance, and afterwards you become regretful to what you have done." (Al-Hujuraat, 6)

So like we said, due to this being a time where many merely follow nothing but their sheer desires, and the people have engrossed themselves in "he said, she said" without verifying as to whether this information is true or not, it becomes even more incumbent to ascertain any information that comes our way before we believe it and before we utter it to others, for sure not doing this leads to one's sure destruction. And Allah grants success!

NOTES

....

....

....

....

....

....

....

....

....

....

....

....

....

....

....

NOTES